# LOST *and* FOUND

## ONE WOMAN'S JOURNEY TO WELLNESS

*Jemma Macera*

**BALBOA**
PRESS

A DIVISION OF HAY HOUSE

Balboa Press books may be ordered through booksellers or by contacting:

Balboa Press
A Division of Hay House
1663 Liberty Drive
Bloomington, IN 47403
www.balboapress.com
1 (877) 407-4847

Because of the dynamic nature of the Internet, any web addresses or links contained in this book may have changed since publication and may no longer be valid. The views expressed in this work are solely those of the author and do not necessarily reflect the views of the publisher, and the publisher hereby disclaims any responsibility for them.

The author of this book does not dispense medical advice or prescribe the use of any technique as a form of treatment for physical, emotional, or medical problems without the advice of a physician, either directly or indirectly. The intent of the author is only to offer information of a general nature to help you in your quest for emotional and spiritual well-being. In the event you use any of the information in this book for yourself, which is your constitutional right, the author and the publisher assume no responsibility for your actions.

Any people depicted in stock imagery provided by Thinkstock are models, and such images are being used for illustrative purposes only. Certain stock imagery © Thinkstock.

Printed in the United States of America.

ISBN: 978-1-4525-9556-6 (sc)
ISBN: 978-1-4525-9558-0 (hc)
ISBN: 978-1-4525-9557-3 (e)
Library of Congress Control Number: 2014906308

Balboa Press rev. date: 9/8/2014

# FOREWARD

This is a story of a wise and wonderful person whose whole life has been lived in Ithaca, New York. I have known Jemma for many years. Her book has a spiritual and insightful approach from which we all can learn. She reveals courage and a spirit that has endured all her life, with its never-ending searching and learning, even when "it" has been almost too painful.

Her quotations from important authors are enlightening, such as, "A person is consistently called upon to create his own future," by Gregory Baum. Or, "Shamans say we heal with dancing, singing, storytelling, and silence."

Jemma's last paragraph in *September of 2003* is a forever treasure: "I still have miles to walk before I am home, perhaps a different therapy, another supplement, whatever. The enthusiasm, joy, energy with which I greet each day is proof to me that I am no longer robbing the bank."

Let us all celebrate.

Jean B. Orear, MSW
Ithaca, New York

There is a quote that says, "A story and its lessons can only be made useful if shared." I believe Jemma Macera's book to be useful to any reader, in the sense that we can all learn something to enhance our own life, through struggle and victory shared by another.

This is a personal story of a woman who chose to face darkness and despair in her own life, only to find the light when she came to understand, and know her true self.

*Lost and Found* offers wisdom from the heart, because it was written by a woman truly gifted with tremendous character, insight, and great optimism. Furthermore, Jemma offers, through this book, a genuine intent to help others understand and appreciate, when we give more attention to the core of our being, there is a greater opportunity for the true self to make itself known.

Jemma is a pure gem of a lady in heart and soul. And, due to incredible courage and perseverance, she was able to break free from her encounters with darkness and despair, and affirm within, the pure joy of living from her true self, that she so graciously treasures.

I am honored to have been a witness to Jemma's story professionally; to know her personally is an even greater gift. [This] book provides inspiration to anyone seeking to live a more meaningful and happier life.

Dr. Christopher J. Meurer, ND, BS<br>Middleton, Wisconsin

Jemma's is an amazing story of courage, perseverance, willingness to explore the unknown, with determination and strength. The honesty of sharing with us what her life was, and the recognition that she must release the past in order to live in the present and to heal on the physical, emotional, mental, and spiritual levels. Yes, her spirit also needed healing.

This is a book for everyone. There are lessons for all of us and inspiration for each of us as we travel our own path. I also enjoyed the history about Ithaca and Jemma's Italian immigrant family.

The message is about taking your life back. When I see Jemma walking about town, or when she talks about going dancing, I am reminded that we each have choices, and she has, we, too, can heal ourselves.

Barbara Coman, Ph.D.<br>Ithaca, NY<br><u>www.heartcenteredresources.com</u>

# A WORD OF THANKS

Without the support and encouragement of the members or the Writers' Association of the Ithaca area, of which I have been a member for over thirty years, I would not be in this hard-won, wonderful place today. This local organization, started in 1935 by a group of women, may be one of the oldest of its kind in this country.

Two women who belong on the National Treasure list are Kate Payne and Mabel Beggs, founders of the Foundation of Light. From them I learned about dowsing, the healing properties of flower essences, and other vibrational therapies such as "growler tapes," which provide healing through sound. The magnificent, priceless library at the Foundation of Light, from which I have benefitted so much, exists as a result of Kate's wisdom and generosity.

My profound gratitude is heaped upon all of those therapists whom I mention in this book. Of them, Jean Orear must be thanked for straightening out my head. I worked with her for a number of years, and am eternally blessed by her help. As well, bushels full of gratitude go to chiropractors Pierre Gremaud, Alton Anabel, Rich Phelps, Bernie Graham, and all their staff. It is with treatments like theirs that I continue to heal. My longtime friend, Dorothy Lonsky, is to be thanked a bunch for telling me about Trager therapy way back in the 1980s, and about Dr. Pierre Gremaud in 1997. Deena Spears, an intuitive whose vibrational intelligence enables her to "hear" discordance in both instruments and in people, has been a virtual lifesaver to both myself and my son Jay. Thanks also go to Steve Singer, Jack Goldman, and Gweneth Warner.

One Saturday evening each month, a group of twenty or more lovely people, some with guitars, others with tambourine, piano, flute, and other instruments, gather at members' homes for *Richy's Sing*. First, we enjoy breaking bread with a potluck dinner and conversation. Then the instruments are tuned, the songbook opens, and the magic begins. While my companions play and sing folk, popular, seasonal, and cultural songs, I listen, relax, absorb the healing vibrations, and bless Richie for organizing this celebration of life. To me, these evenings are a continuation of my Sunday afternoons at home, when the *paisani* came with their guitars; Dad tuned up his guitar and mandolin and the sounds of their Italian songs lifted my spirits.

My way of thanking my parents, Vincenzo and Venere Bortone Macera - for the envious, everyday homemade Italian meals, the beautiful, well-cared-for home, the overflowing closets, bicycles, roller and ice skates, picnics, security, honesty, sobriety, respect for others, intelligence, generosity, and the Sunday afternoon gathering of *paisani*, creating joyful and relaxing afternoons – is to behave likewise.

# CONTENTS

# INTRODUCTION
## Why this book?

First, and most importantly, I wrote this book to share my experiences in a lifelong journey of self- healing. The first half of my adult life I struggled with depression and pain resulting from damage to my coccyx and central nervous system; and in my maturity, with resulting memory loss. In a quest for self-preservation, I became actively engaged in learning about the causes of my disabilities, and in exploring therapies to heal the pain and arrest the dementia. Therefore, here are some suggested treatments that you won't hear about from your typical medical doctor. My beliefs and methods will strike many of you as non-traditional, even strange, approaches to healing. But there's no proof greater than success, and the fact is, I am healing myself. It is a continuing process – the more I heal, the more I realize there is to heal.

My first 30 or so years reflected a traditional Italian upbringing. My parents emigrated from Italy to the U.S. in 1929. They raised me to believe that a woman should be quiet and nurturing, and take care of her home and family. This book describes my journey from conforming to their expectations, through the challenges that took me to a place of great despair and pain, to a search for alternatives, and how those alternatives helped me.

Of this I am certain: everything we experience in life ultimately affects our health for good or ill. This is important to understand, not just in unraveling the mystery of our own diseases, but in reminding us of the impact our actions have on other peoples' lives as well. The body-mind connection is no longer viewed as an interesting theory, but is generally considered to be established fact.

I share my story as confirmation that we are not alone, that the Universe is always willing to work in cooperation with us toward our healing. If I do not share these experiences, I believe my time on this earth will have been wasted. I've learned that sharing and being generous with our truths is self-healing.

Lastly, I was born with the need to write. Coming from an Italian Roman Catholic family, when I read, in Helen Barolini's *The Dream Book*, that there are fewer Italian-American women writers of my generation than any other culture, I began finding even more pleasure in the act of writing—in finding *voice*. Finding voice is an excellent antidote to sickness.

With that said, I invite you to accompany me as I recount a complex journey of experiences through a life of challenge, resulting dis-ease, and ongoing healing.

## BEGIN THE BEGUINE

In 1996, I started thinking about how much I would enjoy taking a writing course, despite my experiences of significant memory loss. The autobiography course offered by the Ithaca College writing department caught my attention. Enrolling as an extra-mural student, I discovered how much I loved being in a formal learning environment again, and decided to write about my on-going healing.

*Doing easily what others find difficult is talent. Doing what is impossible for talent is genius.*
H.F. Amiel

My experiences, as well as from my reading, have taught me that we are all connected energetically. Harming one part of our universe is to harm all parts. For example, moving contaminated soil from one place to another, using harmful chemicals in diapers, clothing, bedding, building materials, farming, manufacturing, water, dentistry, and so-called medicine, are not the activities and beliefs of an intelligent, loving, caring life form. Looking for solutions to memory loss with the use of chemicals or nutrients to treat only the brain is like the definition of insanity: doing the same thing over and over and expecting different results.

My hope—no, my expectation—is that this story will motivate others to examine their belief systems and choices, and the way in which their lives and their energies affect everyone else's. It is also my hope that those of you who read this book will eagerly and gratefully leave any self-confining beliefs and practices, and keep choosing healthier ones. I'm still doing just that. And please, take the children and young adults along with you.

In my list below, of Suggested Behaviors and Qualities Necessary for Wellness, I repeat the word "self-awareness" over and over. That's quite deliberate; it is intended to help us understand how necessary that state of mind is to increasing one's wellness and wholeness.

## Suggested Behaviors and Qualities Necessary for Wellness

1.  *Self-awareness*
2.  Willingness to change
3.  Burning desire to succeed
4.  Perseverance
5.  Forgiveness
6.  Compassion
7.  Gratitude
8.  Belief in the impossible
9.  Flexibility
10. *Self-awareness*
11. Joyful nature
12. Genius code: do what the gifted can't do
13. Eliminate stress/worry
14. Defy our culture, our tribal beliefs
15. Visualize the state of desired wellness
16. Pray in thanksgiving, not in want
17. Pretend
18. Take control, be responsible
19. Ask for help
20. *Self-awareness*
21. Give up belief in failure
22. Remain active
23. Be generous
24. Walk barefoot in the grass
25. Sobriety
26. Unquestionable honesty
27. Love of music, dancing, storytelling and silence
28. Passion
29. Self-hypnosis (autogenesis)
30. Self-awareness, emotional maturity

My overriding desire
for each and every one
is to know nothing is impossible.
Take responsibility for your lives
And don't forget to dance. ~JM

# DOCTOR, DOCTOR, MR. M.D.

Often asked if I have a primary physician, my answers lie in having positioned my bibliography, which follows, in a nontraditional order. The authors and characters of the books I read are my physicians and lifelong friends. Uncle Wiggly and Laura Ingalls Wilder are still favorites. At fifteen I pulled an Eleanor Roosevelt biography off a school library shelf. Reading that she kept a diary, I told myself that I could do that, too. My diary entries, rearranged, have been the source of my poetry over the years, and a significant part of my healing journey.

Later, theologians like Pierre Teilhard de Chardin, psychiatrists, nutritionists, therapists, authors such as Henry David Thoreau, Ralph Waldo Emerson, and many others, became my lanterns of hope and knowledge, lighting the path out of both an unhealthy marriage and religion.

A journal entry of Tuesday. August 20, 2002, captures why I began questioning the traditional western medical model, and seeking answers myself.

> *The day started much too early around 3:00 am, even though I hadn't fallen asleep until almost midnight. The reason for my anxiety and tension is concern about the outcome of the coming day: I have an appointment with a doctor to see if I am correct in my suspicion that I have Alzheimer's disease.*
>
> *I manage to doze off and on till about 6:30. While breakfasting and dressing, my out-of-control mind wonders*

*over and over what questions I will be asked. Where do I get my information? What medications am I taking and why? What else am I doing to help myself?*

*Trying to prepare, I bag all the nutritional supplements and a few of the lighter weight books I had read (since I would be walking to keep my rendezvous with history) and head out.*

The morning was blessedly cool for mid-August, the humidity low, the air refreshing as a morning dip in a pool – unlike the previous week. Even so, I felt I was "losing it," unable to even tell the receptionist my name. Also, the bag of books was heavy, like the weight on my heart of all the brain disorders I hear about in children.

Compared to the comfortable colored chairs, the pictures on the walls, the plants, and the collections of things like paperweights and antique medicine bottles in the offices of alternative practitioners, the examining room to which I was escorted felt like a metallic, airless closet.

My first impression of the doctor was that he seemed unapproachable. Even though I told him several times what I had in the noisy plastic grocery bags, he never asked me about them. Instead, he asked me a few questions, like my age, and how long I'd been experiencing my symptoms. He gave me a memory test, and I tried to cram all the colors, directions, dates, and other details into the empty space in my head. It didn't work. I failed.

Next he suggested a mammogram. I told him it wasn't necessary, that I will never have cancer. He said, "Okay," with no expression on his face, while he recorded my response. When I shared with him that I dowse for answers to such issues, he asked me how to spell "dowse."

Then he told me to schedule an MRI at the hospital so that he would know what parts of my brain were damaged. I agreed, thinking it would be nice to learn my diagnosis was correct.

That ended the appointment. As I paid for it, I felt I'd really wasted my time and money, and that I knew more than he did about memory loss, even though I know very little and couldn't remember what I had learned.

*Walking home, my younger brother slips into memory. It is a Sunday afternoon and we are in the parlor on the couch. Fred, at age ten or eleven, is telling me about his idol, Dr. Albert Schweitzer, and the latest book he is reading about Le Grand Docteur. I read articles about our prison system – how unjust it is, how much work it needs if it is to stop arresting and imprisoning innocent people and to begin treating the inmates better through educational opportunities, therapy, and healthy food. I fear that by the time I am old enough to be able to make a difference, all the challenges will be corrected.* (at this writing at age 77, I say "lotsa luck.")

Calling the hospital the next day to make an appointment, I asked how much an MRI costs. $1200.00 was the answer. I hung up, shocked at how behind the times I was. Since I don't have regular X-rays and other often-recommended procedures, I had no idea how expensive everything had become.

But I did know that parts of my brain were damaged: the amygdala in the Limbic system, which deals with emotions, and my hippocampus, where incoming information is processed. There was no way I could justify spending hundreds and hundreds of tax payers' dollars for information I had already gained by dowsing, which was harmless and had taken five minutes or less to do. I also wondered if the electromagnetic waves of the MRI would further damage my brain cells.

I cancelled the appointment, sadly aware of the ever-increasing ways in which we are all being imprisoned.

The suggestion I did accept was to have my blood tested for diabetes, high blood pressure, cholesterol, vitamin deficiencies and other conditions. Everything was normal except my thyroid. A prescription was recommended which I declined. Having read somewhere that cranberries, grapefruit, strawberries and blueberries are good for the thyroid, I now indulge often. And as I learn to calm down, be more relaxed, take my time, not rush and expect the best, my thyroid is listening.

# BIBLIOGRAPHY: Primary Physicians

Acupuncture Without Needles, J.V. Cerney.
New York: Simon and Schuster, 1974.
*A new home treatment that may bring safe, lasting relief from pain for many ailments.*

Algae to the Rescue!, Abrams, Karl. J.
Studio City, CA: Logan House Publications, 1996.
*Everything you need to know about blue-green algae.*

Anatomy of the Spirit, Carolyn Myss, Ph. D.
New York: Three Rivers Press, 1997.
*An inspirational guide to understanding the chakra systems and emotional healing.*

Apple Cider Vinegar, Bragg, Paul and Patricia, M.D., Ph.D.
Santa Barbara, CA: National Book Network, 2002
*The miracles of apple cider vinegar for a longer, healthier life.*

Bach Flower Remedies, Barnard, Julian.
Essex, England: Avery Publishing Group, Inc., 1979.
*The healing properties of flowers for depression and other conditions.*

Beating Alzheimer's, Warren, Tom.
New York: Avery Publishing Group, Inc., 1991
*Warren claims that mercury fillings caused his memory loss.*

Bee Pollen and Your Health, Wade, Carlson.
New Canaan, CT: Keats Publishing, Inc., 1978.
*Bee pollen is a natural source of vitamin and minerals.*

Beyond Aspirin, Newmark, Thomas and Schulick, Paul.
Prescott, AZ: HOHM Press, 2000.
*The use of ginger and other herbs to reduce inflammation.*

The Biology of Belief, Lipton, Bruce, Ph.D. www.brucelipton.com
Santa Rosa, CA: Mountains of Love/Elite Books, 2005.
*Research that proves, incontrovertibly, that biology's most cherished tenets regarding genetic determinism are fundamentally flawed.*

Body Reflexology, Carter, Mildred and Weber, Tammy.
West Nyack, NY: Parker Publishing Co., 1994
*Healing at your fingertips with acupressure and other healing modes.*

Brain Longevity, Khalsa, Dharma, M.D.
New York: Warner Books, Inc., 1997
*One of the best books for healing memory loss. It is also available on CD.*

Colloidal Silver, Christy, Martha M.
Mesa, AZ: Wishland Publishing Co., Inc., 1998
*The many uses for this antibiotic.*

Colostrum, Lew, Beth M.
Temecula, CA: B.L. Publications, 1997.
*Nature's gift to the immune system.*

The Crazy Makers, Simontacchi, Carol.
New York: Penguin Putnam, Inc., 2000
*How processed food is harming our children.*

Defense Against Alzheimer's, Roberts, H.J., M.D.
   West Palm Beach, FL: Sunshine Sentinel Press, Inc., 1995.
   *A book full of good research and explanations.*

DHEA: Youth and Health Hormone, Shealy, C. Norman, M.D.
   Lincolnwood, IL: Contemporary Publishing Group, Inc., 1999.
   *DHEA is the mother steroid hormone, and is necessary for energy, the immune system, and neurological function.*

Dowsing for Health, Macmanaway, Patrick, M.D.
   New York: Anness Publishing Co., 2001.
   *This book also contains information on Feng Shui.*

The Dream Book, Barolini, Helen.
   New York: Schocken Books, 1985.
   *An explanation of why there are fewer Italian-American women writers of my generation than any other culture.*

Ears of the Angels, Spear, Deena.
   Carlsbad, CA: Hay House, Inc., 2002.
   *I have experienced amazing long-distance healing by Deena.*

Eat Right 4 Your Type, D'Adamo, Peter.
   New York: Putnam, 1996.
   *The individualized diet solution to staying healthy, and living longer.*

Electrical Nutrition, Hiestand, Denis and Shelley.
   Bellevue, WA: Sheldon Corp., 1999.
   *How to use the body's electrical system for healing.*

The Encyclopedia of Dreams, Guiley, Rosemary.
   New York: Berkley Publishing Group, 1998.
   *An excellent book on the symbolism of dreams.*

Energy Medicine, Eden, Donna.
> New York: Penguin Putnam, Inc., 1998.
> *Using our body's energy to stay healthy.*

Energy Nutrition, Howell, Dr. Edmund.
> Wayne, NJ: Avery Publishing Group, Inc., 1985.
> *Unlocking the secrets of eating right for health, vitality, and longevity.*

Enzymes: the Fountain of Life, Lopez, D.A., M.D.; Williams, R.M., M.D., Ph.D., Miehlke, K., M.D.
> Germany: The Neville Press, Inc., 1994.
> *This book is about the relationship between immunology and enzymology.*

Essential Oils: Integrative Medical Guide, Young, D. Gary, D.C.
> Orem, UT: Essential Science Publishing, 2003.
> *Dr. Young went from being told he would never walk again, following an accident, to proving the professionals wrong and creating a whole industry around essential oils and their amazing healing abilities.*

Essential Reiki, Stein, Diane.
> Freedom, CA: The Crossing Press, 1996.
> *A complete guide to an ancient healing art.*

Flower Essences and Vibratinal Healing, Gurudas.
> San Rafael, CA: Cassandra Press, 1983.
> *This book explains how vibrational healing works and also lists the healing properties of many flowers and how to use them.*

Fluoride: The Aging Factor, Yiamouyiannis, John, Ph.D. and John R. Lee, M.D.
> Delaware, OH: Health Action Press, 1993.
> *A well-documented book on the harmfulness of fluoride.*

The Freedom Path, Detzler, Robert E.
> Redmond, WA: SRC Publishing, 1988.
> *This book is about spiritual response therapy and its applications.*

God Helps Those Who Help Themselves, Kroeger, Hanna.
> Boulder, CO: Hanna Kroeger Publications, 1994.
> *Her loving presence pervades this book and all her others.*

The Goddess Path, Monaghan, Patricia.
> St. Paul, MN: Llewellyn Publications, 2002.
> *This book is a guide on your spiritual path. I especially revere the chapters of Quan-Yin, the goddess of compassion.*

Heal Your Body, Hay, Louise L.
> Santa Monica, CA: Hay House, Inc., 1988.
> *What pain in various parts of the body means from an emotional viewpoint.*

Home Coming., Bradshaw, John.
> London: Piotkur, 1990.
> *An autobiographical account of his healing of alcoholism.*

How to Heal Disease With Salt: the Forgotten Wisdom of the Ancient Mariners. Biser, Sam.
> Charlotsville, VA: The University of Natural Healing, Inc., 1994.
> *This report features the life work of Jacques De Langre, Ph.D, a leading proponent in the world for the use of natural ocean salt in our diets.*

Imagery in Healing. Achterberg, Jeanne.
> Boston: Shambala Publications, Inc., 1985.
> *A wonderful book on how imagination can be used for healing and pain reduction.*

Infinite Mind, Hunt, Valerie.
Malibu, CA: Malibu Publishing, 1996.
*The author has done extensive research on non-local energy.*

The International Society for the Study of Subtle Energies and Energy
Medicine, www.issseem.org.

The Isaiah Effect, Braden, Gregg.
New York: Harmony Books, 2000.
*Research from the Dead Sea Scrolls.*

Life Song, Schul, Bill, Ph.D.
Walpole, NH: Stillpoint Publishing, 1994.
*Transcending barriers to interspecies communications.*

Light Beings Master Essences, Schneider, Peter and Pieroth, Gerhard K.
Twin Lakes, WI: Harper Collins Publications, 1997.
*Healing essences from ascended beings.*

Live Better Longer, Dispenza, Joseph.
New York: Harper Collins Publications, 1997.
*Dr. Hazel Parcell's research for health and longevity.*

M.A.P.: The Co-creative White Brotherhood Medical Assistance
Program, Wright, Machaelle Small.
Warrentown, VA: Perelandra, Ltd., 1994
*How to consciously establish a co-creative partnership with nature. Do
not be misled by the word white.*

The Neutraceutical Revolution, Firshein, Richard, D.O.
New York: Penguin Putnam, Inc., 1998
*Twenty cutting edge nutrients to help you design your own whole-life
program.*

<u>Nourishing Traditions,</u> Fallons, Sally with Enig, Mary G., Ph.D.
Washington, D.C.: New Trends Publishers, 1999.
*This book dispels the idea of and challenges "politically correct" nutrition.*
*It includes some great recipes, though I don't agree with the author about*
*disposing of the seeds and skins of perfectly healthy tomatoes!*

<u>O2xygen Therapies,</u> McCabe, Ed.
Morrisville, NY: Energy Publications, 1988.
*Healing unhealable diseases.*

<u>Quantum Healing,</u> Deepak Chopra, M.D.
New York: Bantam Books, 1989.
*Exploring the frontiers of mind-body medicine.*

<u>Releasing Emotional Patterns with Essential Oils,</u> Mein, Caroline, D.C.
Santa Fe, CA: Vision Ware Press, 1998.
*This book is a reference for connecting specific essential oils and reflex*
*points with specific emotional releases.*

<u>Sacred Contracts,</u> Myss, Carolyn.
New York: Three Rivers Press, 2002.
*In coming to know our archetypal companions, we also begin to see how*
*to live in ways that make the best use of our personal power, and lead us*
*to fulfill our greatest potential.*

<u>Seasalts Hidden Powers, De</u> Langre, Jacques, Ph.D.
Magalia, CA: Happiness Press, 1994.
*Details the importance of sea salt in preventing poor mental functioning*
*and dementia.*

<u>The Teachings and History of Tenrikyo: Edited by Translation Section</u>
<u>of Tenrikyo Overseas Mission Department,</u> Tenri, Hara, Japan, Tenry
Jihosha, 1986.
*The life of Miki Nakayama, a 19th-centure Shinto shaman.*

To Kill a Mockingbird, Lee, Harper.
> USA: JB Lippincott Company, 1962.
> *This is my favorite book and a favorite movie. The reference librarian who helped me with this bibliography told me her dog is named Atticus Finch.*

Uncle Wiggly's Story Book, Garis, Howard R.
> USA: The Platt & Munk Co., Inc., 1921.
> *The first book I remember reading: full of moral teachings.*

The Velveteen Rabbit, Williams, Margery.
> Garden City, NY: Doubleday & Company, Inc.
> *An uplifting children's story for everyone.*

Wheat Grass, Meyerowitz, Steve.
> Great Barrington, MA: Sproutman Publications, 1998.
> *The complete guide to using grasses to revitalize your health. The book is full of personal healing stories.*

Why People Don't Heal and How They Can. Carolyn Myss, Ph.D.
> New York: Three Rivers Press, 1997.
> *An exploration of the deep-seated, spiritual causes of illness, and the symbolic lessons that underlie it.*

The Wrinkle Cure, Perricone, Nicholas, M.D.
> New York: Watner Books, 2000.
> *Another book full of interesting research and suggestions.*

Your Inner Physician and You, Upledger, John, D.O., O.M.M.
> Berkeley, CA: North Atlantic Books, 1991.
> *This book is about Cranialsacral Therapy and its healing power.*

Your Own Perfect Medicine, Christy, Martha.
> Scottsdale, AZ: Future Med., Inc., 1994.
> *Read it. You'll be surprised.*

Zinc and Other Micro-Nutrients, Pfeiffer, Carl, M.D.
New Canaan, CT: Keats Publishing, Inc., 1978.
*An invaluable help for staying well.*

# IF I HAD A HAMMER

"If I Had a Hammer" is a Peter, Paul and Mary favorite from the 1960s. Its message of love, peace, and understanding transcends the generations. Perhaps you remember the verses: "If I had a hammer, a bell to ring, a song to sing". . . for me, the pen is my hammer, my bell, and my song.

When I began thinking about writing this book, I entertained the idea of putting my manuscript into boxes, instead of having it bound. My reasoning is that we are all in boxes. It is imperative to examine our individual lives, to ask questions of ourselves. We have to know who we are, how we think and don't think, in order to know where to begin, how to proceed to actually achieve our goals. Changing boxes is a lifelong pursuit. Knowing what to keep is also extremely valuable.

But the complexities, and costs, of putting this book into boxes, have led me to choose a traditional binding.

In compiling this book, I found it easy to relate stories about two contributing factors to my memory loss: damage to my nervous system resulting from an injury to my coccyx and central nervous system, and emotional traumas which caused chemical imbalances in my brain. But thinking about how to recreate the third major factor – the stresses of marriage and motherhood – left me feeling exhausted, confused, and desperately wanting someone to hold my hand, to say, "It's okay, girl, there is no hurry. Rest. Calm down. Time doesn't exist."

You can imagine my breath of joy when a few working dendrites and brain cells reminded me that I have those experiences captured in poetry and memoir.

Blessed be.

## LEARNING TO FLY

I am the pen, the paper,
the thoughts, the memories, the silence,
the pain, the victim.

I am the words, the calm, the peace,
the joy, the light, the forgiveness,
the compassion, the power, the transcendent,
the victor.

I am the magic, the miracle, the unexplainable,
the beginning, the end, the endless,
I am. ~JM

# WE SHALL OVERCOME

People often ask me how it is that I believe in the impossible. I tell them that it is essential to healing oneself. In attempting to shed a bit of light on that, I have to take you back again to the era of Peter, Paul, and Mary.

> *If you don't expect the unexpected you will never find it.*
> – Jurgen Moltmann

After Martin Luther King, Jr. was killed in 1968, Professor Jack Goldman, who was teaching German literature at Cornell University, decided it was time to integrate the city of Ithaca, New York. That was an enormous project for a person to take on. It seemed impossible that he could pull it off.

My family home, where I still reside, is on the edge of the Southside neighborhood in downtown Ithaca, where African Americans, regardless of income or profession, and low-income families, were ghettoized, often in substandard housing.

Jack Goldman formed an organization that addressed these long-standing inequalities in housing. This new group welcomed everyone interested in making real changes in moving and eliminating boundaries between rich and poor, black and white. I joined and worked with Jack Goldman's organization.

MOVE, the name chosen for the organization, is not an acronym; it is a verb chosen because it embodies the spirit of the membership: a commitment to move out old thinking and behavior patterns and replace them with the laws outlined in the Constitution and the Bill of Rights.

As I became acquainted with families that often included four or more children, an occasional grandchild, and a great-grandmother all living together, I became convinced that home ownership was an essential part of the solution. Being in one's own home would end the cycle of constant moving. It would enhance self-respect, teach home-ownership skills, improve neighborhood pride, and more.

But where could I find houses in decent condition, low enough in price and large enough in bedrooms? Again, it seemed like an impossible dream. And there were other huge challenges. I had to find a way to help these families come up with a down payment, closing costs, an attorney, and occasionally extra furniture. Impossible, I thought—until I started listening to an inner voice that told me to "pretend" that I would succeed, that I could find everything each family needed.

*Imagination in more important than knowledge.*
~ Albert Einstein

And I did.

To believe in something is similar to an electrical current charging our battery, strengthening our will. It's like an automatic door opener.

In 1970, MOVE turned itself into Ithaca Neighborhood Housing Services. By 1972, the Human Rights Commission was active; discrimination was illegal. MOVE had accomplished its original goal: to move out old thinking and behavior patterns.

# THE BANK ROBBER

To the question, "Who am I?," I used to answer that I am a bank robber, my self being the bank and my memory being what I stole until it was almost gone.

Now I add descriptive nouns, like *preservationist, glorified janitor,* even *systems-buster.* I can also include *published poet* and *writer.* But I like *janitor* best. It's honest, modest, and truthful. After all, I'm cleaning up old stories, cleaning out forgotten and overlooked concerns of my life and my family's, and preserving them for posterity.

I sweep my mind every day, searching for feelings, ideas, new and fresh ways to capture a moment in eternity. Eliminating clutter in doing so, I am repairing my life, mending friendships, gluing families back together.

Remarkably enough, I am mending my memory, cleaning up brain debris, repairing dendrites, electrical systems, and my central nervous system at a time when professionals are saying it cannot be done. That it's impossible.

 WHO AM I, WHERE AM I, AND DO I LIKE IT HERE?

1. Why?
2. Do drugs heal?
3. Am I sure?
4. Do I ever ask, "Who is paying for the research?"
5. Do I have more than one identity in case of a power shortage?
6. How frugal am I?
7. Why?
8. Do I listen to my eccentricities?
9. Who do I consider a professional?
10. Why?
11. Am I living in the past or the present?
12. How do I know?
13. Who are my models?
14. Why?
15. Am I educated or programmed?
16. How do I know?
17. What do I want to accomplish in my life?
18. Why?
19. What do I want to change?
20. Why?
21. Do I learn from life?
22. Why?
23. What excuses do I use?
24. Do I receive help from unseen sources?
25. How do I know?

26. Who are my friends?
27. Why?
28. What's the healthiest kind of drinking water? Well water. (This is a joke, son!)

# WAKE UP CALL

It's 1997. Walking home from the Ithaca Bakery, where I have gone to buy dough to make pizza, I stop at the corner of West Court and North Geneva Streets, let a car pass, and look up to cross the street. Nothing is familiar. Everything is fuzzy, like an out-of-focus camera. It's as if the Wizard of Oz has rolled in the wrong scene. I live in my hometown, in my family home, and yet I don't recognize anything. What is going on?

I continue looking around, up and down the streets. Nothing clears. I am lost. The street names mean nothing to me. There is not one familiar house. I stay there on the corner, thinking the fuzziness will clear up. It does not.

I tell myself to remain calm. To remember. I have walked these streets thousands of times. If I continue walking, I will find the Yellow Brick Road again.

Eventually, houses and churches register in my exhausted, starved brain.

Over the years, I've been lost, and found myself, many times. The more found you are, the more you know you were lost.

## Cast of Characters

| | |
|---|---|
| Vincenzo Macera, father | January 22, 1894 – May 5, 1956 |
| Venere Bortone, mother | August 12, 1902 – February 17, 1973 |
| Mary Macera, sister | August 7, 1930 |
| James Macera, brother | August 11, 1932 – January 26, 2007 |
| Jemma Macera | July 31, 1935 |
| Fernando (Fred) Macera | November 18, 1932 – August 15, 2004 |
| Frederick T. Wilcox, husband | August 8, 1932 – November 4, 1982 |
| Frederick Thomas Wilcox III, son | October 19, 1954 |
| Shannon Wilcox, daughter | October 31, 1956 |
| Jay Joseph Wilcox, son | January 6, 1962 |
| B. Kelly Wilcox, son | September 12, 1963 |

 THE TWELFTH OF NEVER

Wanting to find out as much as I could about my parents' lives in Fondi, Italy, before they became my parents, I visited one of my mother's friends, who still lived in the same house to which her husband brought her, here in Ithaca, New York, in the 1920s. She was doing quite well at eighty-nine, despite arthritic legs.

Laura Battisti's English is better than mine; she learned to drive at sixty-five, and she's not fanatical about her religion. Another reason for my respect and affection for Laura is that she encouraged me to pursue my writing interests. Even though she was born in a different town than my parents, Laura was able to turn many of my question marks into periods and exclamation points. I am eternally grateful. The first time visiting her, I showed her my collection of Mom's linen towels, two with crocheted borders that spell out *Buon Giorno* and *Venere Bortone*. They now hang in my bathroom with a small, hand-printed sign that says: *Keepa You Hands Off*.

I told Laura about my grandfather, who wore velvet suits and talked to his horses in French, blamed his wife for their eldest son's choice of a bride and stopped talking to her. The silence lasted ten years, until she died when Mom, Venere Bortone, was sixteen. In reality, Mom lost both parents, because her father spent his days and nights in the cantinas and wouldn't let her out of the house, which was not unusual at that time. Even though Mom was born into a very wealthy family—Vincenzo Bortone owned the water rights of his village Fondi—I remember her telling me that she had to make some clothing out of her brothers' shirts.

On the other hand, Dad, who had only two years of schooling, had

25

to work, perhaps as a shepherd, and save his lire in order to fulfill his plan to emigrate to America with his step-brother Benedetto. In fact, Dad had to save his lire twice. Giving his earnings into his mother's keeping was not the best plan of action. She used the money to buy *vino*. Instead of giving up, Dad again saved his earnings and kept them himself. I now wonder what Benedetto's experience was.

When Vincenzo Macera first arrived in his new world of Ithaca, New York in 1912, he was eighteen years old and totally responsible for his survival. One of his jobs was laying track for the railroad the enterprising Speno family was building on Ithaca's East Hill. The Speno family sponsored many Italian immigrants, but not my Dad.

In 1915, Dad and Benedetto returned to Fondi to join the Italian army. Having the choice of enlisting in either country's military, my guess is that Dad chose Italy so that he could visit his mother, his sisters Rosalia and Lucia, and any friends he had.

While telling Laura what I knew about my parents, I gave her some Concord grapes from the grapevine Dad had planted on the border between our house and the house next door. While Laura enjoyed the gift, I thought of the apple trees Dad planted back in the '40s, and how easy he made it look to graft three other species of apples. And I thought of the potatoes and rats that kept him alive in the Hungarian prisoner of war camp in 1916 and 1917.

So, I told Laura, Dad stayed in Italy until 1920, traveling and probably working. He also returned to Fondi, where he met my mother Venere. When he returned to Ithaca, he worked on the new heating plant and the Arts Quad for Cornell University, and that by 1923 he had saved enough money to buy both his mother's home in Fondi for $2,000 and a house at 303 South Plain Street in Ithaca for $2,500. Benedetto was married by then, living two doors down at 307 South Plain, and the two of them were bootlegging during Prohibition. I said I was impressed by how frugal Dad was, and then asked Laura if she knew how Dad had met Nellie, his *Mantenuta* (common law wife).

Laura leaned forward in her dark blue 1950s-style overstuffed living room chair. I sat across from her, watching her eyes change color as the afternoon light faded across her smooth face. Her yellow-and-white checkered housedress brought a bit of sun and warmth into the room and into me. Time tiptoed backward and forward as Laura's voice transported me to other worlds. Forward and backward.

"My husband and your father were friends," she told me, "and Nellie and my husband's first wife, who later died, were also friends. But Nellie was too '*Americana*.' She drank too much and complained if your father brought his friends home to dinner. She didn't want to spend her money or time on his friends. Your father tired of her, so he wrote to his mother, asking about the single women in the village.

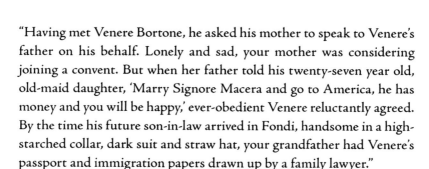

# WEDDING BELLS

"Having met Venere Bortone, he asked his mother to speak to Venere's father on his behalf. Lonely and sad, your mother was considering joining a convent. But when her father told his twenty-seven year old, old-maid daughter, 'Marry Signore Macera and go to America, he has money and you will be happy,' ever-obedient Venere reluctantly agreed. By the time his future son-in-law arrived in Fondi, handsome in a high-starched collar, dark suit and straw hat, your grandfather had Venere's passport and immigration papers drawn up by a family lawyer."

"Where was the religious wedding?" I remembered hearing something about two ceremonies.

"Whenever your grandfather drank too much, he became mean and loud. Your mother was afraid he would spoil the day if she had a big church wedding as her sister Giuseppina did."

"Oh yes," I interrupted. "I remember Mom saying that her father had sand spread all over the cobblestone streets. That was done so that the horses wouldn't slip pulling the carriages. The wedding was held at home and the civil ceremony took place at City Hall," Laura explained.

Fondi, which dates back to the Middle Ages, lies north of the port of Naples. I can see the newlyweds being jostled in the horse-drawn carriage that took the sad-eyed bride, her stranger of a groom, and the huge wooden trunk of *biancheria* (linens) to the ship. I wonder if her sisters, Gemma, Giuseppina, and Celeste, and her brother, Vincenzo, accompanied her, thinking that could be the last time they would see her. Fortunately, they were all literate, so letters did cross the Atlantic.

How I wish Mom had saved those early confessions, as she did the decades-later ones I now cherish. There are no letters from Luigi, her older brother. Mom was angry at Luigi her whole life. She felt he urged their father to agree to the marriage to get rid of her. Once she was here in America, he would have her share of the inheritance.

Laura M. Battisti was born August 4, 1909. She died September 5, 2001.

I miss her.

 COMING TO AMERICA

After a weeklong journey across the Atlantic Ocean, Venere and Vincenzo Macera pass through Ellis Island, where they are examined for contagious diseases and for passports. The term *WOP* comes from those times, and stands for *without passport*. I still have both my parents' passports in my possession.

Leaving New York City, Dad brings Mom directly to Ithaca to his house at 303 South Plain Street. The time is October 1929. The Great Depression has just begun.

As Mom looks around the matchbox-size wooden houses on South Plain, packed together like spaghetti, and sees for the first time dark-skinned people dressed in clothes she would not have used to mop the kitchen floor, she becomes frightened. In Fondi the houses are made of stone and marble. *"Dio mio,"* she prays over and over. *"Where has this man brought me?"* She wonders if she has been taken down from a cross of loneliness to be put back up on another of hunger.

An enterprising man, Dad had worked constructing buildings up on the hill at Cornell University. Now he is bootlegging. From Mom I learned that he used her dowry money to buy more equipment. Honest and sober, he pocketed the extra nickels for future plans—like buying his wife a wringer washing machine, something very few working-class families could afford during those years.

Cops and other respectables came to South Plain Street to buy a glass of beer. "Of course the cops came," my sister Mary told me. "How else could they gather proof that Dad was engaged in illegal activities so that they could arrest him?" For someone unaccustomed to dealing with the public, let alone with the police, it must have been a terrifying experience for Mom to bail Dad out of jail.

That wasn't all Mom had to endure. One day a cop came in to ask for a glass of beer. Since Dad was at work, Mom waited on him. She noticed that he left a little beer in the glass. No one had ever done that before. A short time later the cop returned to arrest her. Mary was less than two and Mom was pregnant with my brother, Jim. What was she to do? She started pointing to her belly, making guttural sounds, and between that and her Italian and broken English, she communicated her situation. The cop gave up and left. There were plenty of others in the neighborhood making moonshine, so it probably didn't matter that one bootlegger got away.

For the next couple of years, the little house with uneven floors, which Mom hated, was a significant partner in Dad's plans for himself and his family. It was not only the birthplace of my siblings Mary and Jim, and the factory that bottled homemade brew, it was also a little grocery store. While other men were out drinking or gambling, or even dallying, Dad was out—after working all day at the Morse Chain factory or for the city for twenty cents an hour—walking blocks and blocks to buy goods and other grocery items he could mark up by a penny or two. Dad also spent his lunch hour at home straightening nails so he could reuse them and pieces of wood for the needed home repairs.

Because Venere was female-born, she served a life sentence of loneliness and mind-destroying unfulfilment. She was a lovely woman in her youth. But her mother probably never told her so, not once. After all, there were ten births in her mother Peppina's marriage—six living, four dead. No time to tell your daughter how lovely her dark, wavy hair was, or how bright her dark brown eyes are. There was time, however, to tell her young sad daughter not to sit in a chair immediately after someone else—especially if it was a man. Why? Babies.

There was time to teach her to carry the water, wash her brothers' clothes, tend to the younger children. Venere finished the fourth grade. Nine years old when she became a housewife. Trapped into servitude to her father and brothers.

When the news broke that Prohibition might soon be repealed, Federal agents spread out in the neighborhoods urging the lawbreakers to get legal. They advised the bootleggers to rent or buy a building and open up a bar. Watering holes would be greatly needed, meeting places on a work night or Saturday night, to gather with fellow laborers, relax over a pint and a Limburger cheese sandwich. (I can still hear Mom's words of complaint. Limburger cheese smells like rotten vomit and its odor clings to anything it can—hands, clothing, hair, air, even nothing at all.)

> *The first lesson of history is to learn the goodness of evil.*
> —Ralph Waldo Emerson

The agents urged the immigrants to think ahead. Mom and Dad listened. After talking it over, they decided that they could open a restaurant with Mom as chef if the news about repealing Prohibition turned out to be premature. Dad sold the house at 303 South Plain Street and used the money toward the down payment on a brick building on the corner of East Green and South Tioga streets, which had formerly belonged to the Fraternal Order of Eagles. Of the $15,000 purchase price, Dad was given a $12,000, five-year mortgage to be paid twice annually.

Part of the second floor of the building was converted into living space for my parents and my sister and brother—and eventually me, when I was born in 1935. The other rooms and the whole third floor accommodated guests by the night, week, or month. How an Italian immigrant came up with the name—Jim's Oriental Hotel —is still a mystery to me. I hated the name. It embarrassed me. Years and years later I was told Dad liked exotic names.

But that and his license to sell alcohol brought a constant, committed troop of construction workers, carpenters, painters, and factory employees eager to plunk their nickels down for a glass of beer. Evenings, bands played country music, couples danced; beer, whisky and conversation flowed.

I wonder if Mom knew about Nellie, her husband's former common-law wife. Even so, what a shock it must have been the day Nellie and her sister and brother-in-law showed up at the hotel, asking for jobs. They were from Auburn, a town some 30 miles away. Nellie must have heard from her friends in Ithaca that Dad was doing well, and she hoped he would help them out.

Totally against Mom's wishes—"they'll steal from you"—not only did Dad hire Nellie as a waitress, he gave all three of them bedrooms. Nellie was totally different from her sister, who was on the heavy side, quiet, plain as white rice with no salt or pepper. She worked only when Nellie wasn't well. Nellie was a firecracker. Henna-dyed and permed hair, makeup and tight dresses, a glass of beer in one hand and a cigarette in the other. Sometimes even something as thin as air couldn't have passed between her and the "gentleman" to whom she served a 5-cent beer or a 1-cent Hershey's chocolate bar. Her brother-in-law, who was considered a pain in the neck, was thin and pale-faced. A cigarette always a fixture between his lips and a beer glass always near, he tended bar. Just as Mom predicted, the two of them were caught pocketing money that should have been in the cash register.

In the winter of 1936 or '37, Nellie's brother-in-law became too ill to work. What puzzled Mom, whenever she was out shopping or taking me for a walk, were the open windows to his bedroom. No matter how often she closed them, she found them open again. One cold, snowy, black-topped-sky day, seeing the shivering curtains and the snow blowing in, she again went to close the window, and saw the brother-in-law's ashen-faced, motionless body in the bed.

My sister Mary related all this to me, and she doesn't remember what happened to Nellie and her sister. The brother-in-law died. I found out years later from the son of my parents' friends, that they believed Nellie and her sister were responsible for opening the windows and hastening his death.

* * *

Dear Nellie,

Does it feel as though I've rudely shaken you awake, dragged you out of the darkness, filled you with nine-volt batteries and turned on the switch? It feels that way to me. Don't run away or hide your face, I want to thank you.

What a blessing to meet again, after all this time. There's no memory of you when I was an infant, even though we lived in the same building, passed in the hallway, and you probably smiled at me and touched my fingers or wiggled my toes and asked Mom if I was teething or talking. You were, and still are, like a breeze—unseen but remembered.

The small silver jewelry box, with the spread-winged eagle and your name on the top that Dad bought from you when you were selling your possessions while you lived and worked at the hotel, is how I learned of your existence. It was kept on Mom's dresser, here in our Green Street home, and I used to look inside and play with the necklaces and earrings.

I want to thank you for being a friend, companion, lover, to my father. Even though he was very intelligent, smart, honest and hardworking, "polite" society was closed off to him. The only role allowed him was that of a laborer. You saw him as someone of value, and I'm grateful.

I have so many questions. Did you and your sister really kill your brother-in-law? What happened to you after you left? Did you ever stop drinking? Remarry? Change? Believing what I now do, we will meet again so you can fill me in.

\* \* \*

Learning more about Nellie has piled higher and higher the understanding, appreciation and gratitude I have for my mother. In the following chapters, I share my dislike for her, in part because she did not have a value system I could embrace. What I've also recorded is the place of great peace to which I have arrived through examination, understanding, resolution, and desire to ease on down the road.

# HERE I'LL STAY

I was about three years old when we moved two blocks from Jim's Oriental Hotel to the house I live in today. It is a brick Italianate. The stone steps that reminded Mom of Fondi, and sunlight on the gorgeous carved golden double doors, must have struck a smile in her dark eyes as Dad showed her the two-story brick mansion with a For Sale sign in the yard.

Inside, she loved everything. Eleven-foot ceilings, two marble fireplaces, big windows, a large kitchen with an enclosed porch, a six-room basement for canning tomatoes, peaches and pears, and for washing clothes and drying them in bad weather. There was also room to kill chickens and goats.

Mom continued looking around, no doubt thinking, *No more lugging babies, strollers, and groceries up and down long flights of stairs; there's grass for the children, garden space for roses and lily-of-the-valley, a two-story front porch for resting on a hot summer's evening. Mamma mia, che grazie.* God had answered her prayers.

Looking at the hardwood floors, Dad may have been reminded of the dirt floor of his childhood home back in Fondi, and felt pleased with his achievements.

\* \* \*

When Dad approached Judge Fitz Stephens and told him in very good English that he wanted to buy his house, the judge, seeing a spaghetti-bender, a WOP, wondered how Dad was going to pay for it. Pulling $7,000 out of his pocket, Dad asked for and received a $3,000 five-year mortgage. The payments were due twice yearly, April 1st and October 1st. Any default on Dad's part, and both the money and the house would revert back to Judge Stephens. Apparently the judge was expecting this to happen, because when Dad showed up to pay the final $3000, he refused to accept it. Now I know why Mom spoke so highly of Edward Casey, the attorney Dad hired to make Judge Stephens honor their agreement. None of this information came from Dad; he never spoke ill of anyone.

Because it was purchased as a single-family home, the house's main bathroom was on the second floor. Dad converted our kitchen pantry into a bathroom, and one of the upstairs rooms into a kitchen, and rented out the six-room upper apartment to a widow, Carmella Velletri, and her children. Carmella's husband died in the flu epidemic in 1917, so she returned to Italy for a while, working as a seamstress. By the early 1930's, the depression in Europe was terrible, and Hitler and Mussolini rose to power. Carmella sent her American-born son back to the United States because, as an American citizen, he could send for her and her

Italian-born daughter to return to the safety of America. Carmella, always in black, was a lovely, intelligent, genteel woman. I especially liked her because it was her hands that caught me that hot July day when I was born.

Our house was on a corner. There was lawn on all sides. And flowers. Dad was prosperous enough that Mom could have rose bushes and lily of the valley and peonies growing around the house. Everything didn't have to be turned into a vegetable garden. He did border our property with two grape vines that still produce more grapes than I can eat and that give me an opportunity to be generous. As he was. And, at one time, he planted an apple tree, on which he grafted five different species of apple. Years and years later I learned to appreciate the skill it takes to make such endeavors successful.

\* \* \*

Moving back into the family home in 1979, and even though a new kitchen sink might make life easier for me now, I wouldn't exchange the slightly pockmarked porcelain one for all the Italian fruitcake in the world. It and the black-and-white enamel table with the black leather and chrome chairs, the kitchen armoire made by Enorfino Cicchetti, that stores dishes on the top shelves, and gallon cans of Fillipo Berio olive oil and one-pound boxes of macaroni below (instead of the five-pound boxes Mom bought) preserve a feeling of comfort and unpretentiousness my friends and I appreciate.

At the end of the twentieth century I sadly replaced the monstrous converted gas boiler with a new, more efficient, and smaller unit. What has not changed is the banging, exploding, and tapping sounds the steam makes as it courses through the same pipes and radiators Dad had installed. In Morse code I am being told all is well in this house. I am loved, warm, safe.

# TO SIR WITH LOVE

I always liked to say that my father was short for his age. Darker than Mom, but not as dark as some other Italians who come to visit, he looks healthy, ruddy maybe. He never has a belly.

I like the way he walks; not arrogant because he has to pretend; not shy because he is an Italian immigrant and might be considered dishonest, or not sober, or unemployed. He walks with delight for being here in America. He walks with the satisfaction of knowing his children go to school well-dressed and better-nourished than anyone. He walks with the pride of having purchased a magnificent house for his wife and family. No one he or his family encounters has a finer home. Paid for with rectangular-shaped paper.

What shape are security and honesty and sobriety and hard work? I feel those shapes around me, still. Years after his death they are my currency. I go anywhere and everywhere with them.

\* \* \*

School mornings, if Dad were up while I was on my way out the door, our fifteen seconds of meaningful time together consists of just two words:

"*Come stai?*" he asks

"*Molto bene,*" is my non-varying reply.

*Molto bene* (very well). How I enjoy saying those two words. They transport me to another world of marble and cobblestones and

Renaissance art. I am an angel for a few seconds in one of Giotto's paintings. Dad said that Giotto could draw a perfect circle freehand.

If Dad were home on a rare afternoon when he could rest, he sat in the living room by the bay window, smoking a Camel cigarette, his hair still jet black, his pants always blue, his shirt always white. If I were headed out somewhere," Watch your step," he warned me in English. Those words were his hugs and kisses.

\* \* \*

Hanging on one of my living room walls today, in a 1920s frame, is an enlarged black and white photograph of Dad and four other Italian musicians, two with guitars, two with mandolins, like Dad's. He also had a guitar, but it was not at all flashy. No reds and greens and sparkles. It was brown. Ordinary brown. Buster Brown shoe polish brown. What I can remember most, however, is his mandolin.

Of all the Sunday afternoon visits with other *paisani*, I remember the song-playing and singing the most fondly. Whenever I asked, Dad played my favorite song and sang it, and I don't recall his having a song sheet.

\* \* \*

## FIRST CRUSH

He was much older than I.
Short, stocky, with shiny, witch-black hair,
a permanent suntan, always dressed
in blue pants, white shirt, polka-dot tie.
Going for walks, how important and safe
I felt holding his hand.
I mimicked him, my feet pointing outward
instead of straight ahead.
A kind neighbor woman taught me otherwise.

Musician friends, with guitars and mandolins,
often gathered at home
for a Sunday afternoon of self-entertainment.
I loved listening to him sing my favorite,
"When The Caissons Go Rolling Along."

He didn't criticize me for wearing sandals or shorts,
though he thought it immodest
when my older sister did.
No matter what I wanted,
he gave it to me, including giving me away
the morning I married.
Years later I took back his name,
  preferring it above the other.

\* \* \*

Thinking of my father sitting in a tan imitation leather chair by the
bay window, I now understand why I plant ivy in a 32 oz. tomato can
with the label still intact. A tin can doesn't belong on a marble-top table,

what's the matter with you? Oh, but it does! It reminds me of my roots, from where I have come, the distance I have traveled and that I haven't traveled. It reminds me of how proud Dad must have been, knowing what a fine house he provided his wife and children. We were not crowded in a stinking, airless tenement in New York City. We were not even on a street here in Ithaca where, through the open window, one could look into the next home, see and hear everything that was going on—like live TV today.

\* \* \*

As a teenager, whenever I want something, a soda or an ice cream, and don't want to ask Mom for fear she will say I don't need it, I go up to see Dad at his hotel. I almost always find him alone in the dining room, reading the Ithaca Journal and smoking. A low-maintenance man, he smokes just half a cigarette at a time. He has no use for a car—what are legs for?

Nice girls don't go into bars, even if their fathers own them. I feel very uncomfortable, out of place, ashamed, like a cheap broad, using the dining room entrance. But necessity overrides my shyness.

"Hi Dad."

No matter what I want, Dad pulls out a huge wad of bills (he carries too much money for a wallet) and gives me what I ask for.

"Thanks, Dad. See you later."

I appreciate the hotel for another reason. Kitty-corner from it is Wool-Scotts Bakery. They make the best five-cent sweet rolls there, inside a warehouse-sized building, where stacks and stacks of white bread wait to be packaged and delivered.

"May I have a sweet roll?" I ask the white-aproned man behind the counter. "Charge it to my father."

Dad never hugs or kisses me, nor tells me that he loves me, but letting me charge a sweet roll is all the proof I need. Neither do I recall Dad ever looking at my report card or giving me a birthday or Christmas gift. But I know it is his efforts that allow Mom to buy the dolls and skates and bikes and swimming lessons, and a new bedroom set and Girl Scout camp and a closet full of nice clothes.

Throughout my childhood, he is my jewel and my jeweler. He still is.

**Afternoon Delight**

Decades and decades ago
In the bakery across from Dad's hotel
"Charge it to My Father," I say,
picking out a sweet roll as thought it were communion.
Eating it I feel like altar linen-
No artificial starch needed. Times change
Buildings like promises come and go.
Watching the new Mental Health Center displace
my childhood fantasies, I wonder
How many therapists will taste sweet rolls
with their clients? ~JM

\* \* \*

Back in the "wiggly years," when I am too young to sit still for more than fifteen minutes or to attend Mass alone, Mom occasionally takes me, much to her regret. Her complaints are numerous. I bang the underside of the pew with my shoes. I touch all the missals in the bookrack, pulling them out and opening them, turning their pages, when I can't even read. I ask too many questions, and I move around too much, including looking back at the silent people in the rows behind me. In short, I am an embarrassment.

Dad doesn't go to Mass. He considers Christians hypocritical. But one Sunday he comes to my rescue. He wants to find out who is right—Mom or me—because of course I think I am the perfect child. When the two of us return home, he proclaims that I behaved very well.

# SUNDAY WILL NEVER BE THE SAME

I remember liking Mom's shape. Not round and fat, nor slim-waisted and pretty like some mothers I know. She is rectangular. Her front and back are longer than her sides. I never feel embarrassed by Mom's ample bosom and her lack of height. She knows how to dress, always corseted and in nylons, with sturdy black tie-shoes because of her bad back. She has wonderful taste when it comes to clothes, especially for Mass. Wintertime, in her Persian lamb coat, a hat covering her coiled black braids she has pinned on top of her head, wearing her shiny school-marmish Sunday shoes, she is one proud woman.

"Where do you work-a-John?" On the Delaware-Lackawann.
"What do you do-a-John?" I poosh I poosh I poosh.
"What do you poosh-a-John?" I poosh I poosh a-da-broom.
~ Anonymous

Accustomed to carrying water from a well, Mom was a miser. Monday mornings the classic healing smell of beef or chicken soup perfumed the kitchen, bubbling on the battleship-size stove that took up practically the whole wall. That left Mom free to devote her energies to hanging out a wash that smelled as clean as an autumn day—before cars polluted the air and sprayed greasy-grimy dirt over everything.

Down in the cellar, surrounded by built-in tubs and piles of laundry, she first washed the white and colorfast clothes. Next, she washed the non-bleachable clothes: our skirts, dresses, blouses, my brothers' shirts, Dad's bar jackets, etc. While they washed, she had the white clothes soaking in a tub with Clorox bleach. In the same wash water, after she had moved the colored clothes into a second tub of clean rinse water, Mom washed the dark things: pants and socks. Emptying the washing machine, she filled it again to rinse the clothes—in the same order, of course.

Some time in the 1950s we finally convinced Mom to buy an automatic washer. She had it installed in the kitchen, between the sink and the window, but she could never fully appreciate it; it wasted too much water. At that time, water was around $3.00 for three months. Mom's attempt to correct the extravagance by overloading the machine ended with her burning out the motor. We convinced her to buy another. When I had my own home and my own Frigidaire washer, I felt guilty that I didn't use the wash water over and over. I could use it to mop the basement floor or scrub the basement steps or the lawn furniture or the garbage cans. I must admit, sometimes I did. And still do.

\* \* \*

I like her best in the kitchen, the long broom-handle rolling pin a natural extension of her hands. She is strong. She knows how to feed an army, and does it well, rolling out dough for macaroni, ravioli, lasagna, or pizza dough for Friday dinner, or dough for twelve apple pies.

During holidays, the twenty-five pound bag of flour is brought out, plus the dozens of eggs, the honey, almonds, sugar, yeast, anise seeds and more, depending on whether it is Lent, Easter, or Christmas. Mom makes hundreds of loaves of Easter bread that she gives to neighbors, friends, priests, nuns, and probably others. The same with Christmas cookies. I make eight or ten loaves of Easter bread and think I'm wonderful, carrying on a family tradition.

Winters, I help her make sausage by grinding the Boston butts that a butcher cuts from the whole pig she buys, and by turning the handle that forces the salt-and-coriander-spiced meat into the casings. Mom also makes her own prosciutto, hanging the salted, peppercorn-covered ham out in the enclosed porch off the kitchen, where it is cured.

# LA BELLA FIGURA, Part 1

Our winter coats, boots, and anything else we needed were always purchased after the holidays or at a sale. That Mom often came home with several blouses and dresses was testimony to her love for a bargain. To make a good impression is very important in the Italian scheme of things. It's called *la bella figura*. We dressed up for the doctor, dentist, lawyer and the priest for that reason. But there was another reason. It was very important to show respect for authority, for educated people, for people to whom you turned in time of need.

*La Bella Figura* was evident in our lives all the way down to the color of the thread used to darn socks. Just home from the hospital, I've lost count which operation it was, Mom spent an afternoon sitting in her rocker by the kitchen window, taking out all the stitches in the socks Louise, our maid, had mended while she was in the hospital being mended. Then she spent the rest of the day darning the holes with the same color thread as the socks.

Never were we without a button or with a rip. Our white clothes were white and our colored clothes were bright.

When I was fifteen, I let Mom buy me a mouton fur coat on sale. I didn't like it, and I couldn't wear it very much since none of my friends had one, not even the store owner's daughter, who was my classmate. But Mom loved it. She was such an unhappy wife, I said yes to please her. "Is that a mink coat?" I was asked. "No it's just mouton," I'd answer, making the word sound ordinary, like grass.

* * *

## DO NOT LOOK FOR HER

Do not look for her there by the grave stone with her name
on it.
She is not there.
Instead you will find her in the rocking chair by the kitchen
window.
In her house dress of brown or blue, she spreads her lap wide
and cleans the dandelion greens that are piled there that she
picked only a few hours ago.

Do not look for her under the dryer at the beauty shop.
She's never been there.
Instead you will find her with jet black braids around her
head, rosary in hand as she waits for the water to boil over the
eight quarts of tomatoes out of the hundred she canned today.

Do not look for her in a taxi cab being taken as a lady of her
class should, to some exciting party.
She always said they were a waste of money.
Instead you will find her at a sale buying
a dozen pair of socks for my brothers,
three dresses for me
and three for Mary
and two dozen pairs of shoes for her family in war-torn Italy.

Do not look for her out dancing on a cool Saturday night.
She's never been.
Instead you will find her on her black-and-white-checkered
kitchen floor, making sauce as only she could for Sunday
  dinner on the morrow.

Do not look for him in bronze and mahogany and a granite stone for a pillow.
He had no use for them.
Instead you will find him walking beside every man.
He found them all to have value.

Do not look for him in some other bar drinking his sorrows away.
He's never been there.
Instead you will find him in an attorney's office paying cash for three houses he just bought.

Do not look for him on a street corner idling the time away.
He never learned how to do that.
Instead you will find him at the post office mailing back the $10.00 he had to borrow to come to the land with the golden door.
Do not look for him at the racetrack betting on a sure thing.
He wouldn't understand the philosophy of that sort of thing.
Instead you will find him playing with me for a little while before he goes back to the restaurant until one a.m.
~ JM

\* \* \*

One morning in 1939, pregnant with her fourth child, Mom tripped over the cat and fell down the basement steps, breaking her tailbone. Mary said it was a compound fracture. I cringe when I think of the suffering Mom must have endured while waiting out the pregnancy to have the corrective surgery. Fernando, "Fred," was born November 19th, and since he was nursing, he accompanied Mom to the hospital for her operation some time later. The other three of us, Mary, Jim and I, were cared for by Mom's friends while she was hospitalized.

Mary remembers coming home for lunch one day, just after Mom had returned home from the hospital, and seeing her leaning against the stove like a fallen branch, using the stove for support. Holding my baby brother with her left arm, she was stirring something for lunch with her right hand. Louise, Mom's maid, should have been there to help her, but she was drunk, three sheets to the wind, a basket case, unable to work. Sandwiches and canned corn were still four-letter words to Mom— unacceptable for her family—until we Americanized her years later.

# SKIP A ROPE

I couldn't wait to learn how to write. One of my early memories is of the sun, warm and splashing through the bedroom window, turning the hardwood floor the color of Golden Delicious Apples. I'm sitting on that floor, making squiggly lines with a pencil on white paper. I'm trying to teach myself the alphabet. The lines all look alike; I can't tell A from B or C. Dad is always working or too tired to ask. Mom can't read or write English. It doesn't occur to me to ask my sister. After several attempts, confusion darkens the room. Nothing to do but wait 'til I'm old enough to go to school.

* * *

Jimmy Frederico has magic in his hands. At five and six years old, I worry that he will leave some day—and then who will take the terrible pain away?

It comes often, the pain. Like one of Mom's headaches, only in my stomach. We are all living on Green Street. Now, in the early 40s, Mom has her mansion, her roses, her rosary. I have my doll, my friend, Lucy Anne. Dad has his hotel, his bar, and his bartender Jimmy. Jimmy has Louise, who I think is his wife, and whom I love 'cause she loves me.

Jimmy can make the horrible pain go away.

It's a warm summer evening. I'm complaining again. Must be suppertime, 'cause Dad is home. Mom is probably busy cooking. It is decided that Dad will take me by the hand up to the hotel, two blocks away. I like walking with my father. The pain doesn't seem so bad when just he and I are together. I even skip a little—I can be happy 'cause Jimmy is going to make everything right again.

As Dad and I walk up Green Street, we pass Miss Wilkinson's stone mansion and the two others just like it. On the second block there are bars, a clothing store, a car dealer—none of interest to me. All that matters is that I am with my father and soon my stomachache will be gone. Then I will feel like playing with my rubber doll that has the gray fur coat and hat and muff. I just love her. I found her under the tree on Christmas Eve.

In the hotel dining room, where we are not observed, Jimmy squats down and has me lie across his knees. He pulls up my dress, makes the sign of the cross over my stomach, and rubs it.

Soon the pain is gone. How does he do it? I wonder. Will he always be here when I need him? By the time I am in third grade, eight years old, the stomachaches are gone. Depression is settling in for a long-term relationship.

But I do not know that then. I am just happy my stomach no longer hurts.

\* \* \*

Growing up, I had an excellent memory and did well in school. Well, that's almost true. There are six U's (Unsatisfactory) on my kindergarten report card. It seems I could not carry my chair quietly.

Graduating in the top 50 in a class of over 280, I wonder how I might have done had I studied occasionally—especially since I was a child of Italian immigrants in a class of students from university families. (After all, many years later I managed a *magna cum laude* A.S. Degree while divorced, seriously depressed, and managing four children and four houses—two family homes and two income properties.)

\* \* \*

In seven years at Henry St. John School, I clearly remember asking only one question of my teacher. She is putting a true-or-false test on the blackboard. We are to answer *yes, no*. I ask why she doesn't write *yes or no*. She tells me it's because some of the students will answer *or*.

How thrilling it feels to be treated like an intelligent person. Those words straighten my shoulders, raise my head, brighten my eyes. For once I am significant, not a sheep in a herd. I am given an explanation instead of being told to just have faith; to just do as I am told.

\* \* \*

My sixth grade teacher, Mrs. Ernestine Banford, is my all-time favorite. What I sense in her is goodness and concern for all students, regardless of color or ethnic background. Not pretty, her dark hair flat on her head, she dresses plainly, like a Sunday school teacher, and she is as patient as my father. When she hangs up an abstract chalk drawing of mine, she cements my love and respect. As long as I live, she lives.

I don't understand why I remember the school janitor, Mr. Elston. He did not rescue me from a burning school or adjust my desk, but he did smile and say hello when we passed in the clean halls. I see him in gray work pants and shirt, retrieving balls off the roof, or shoveling snow.

\* \* \*

Jerry Della Femina begins his autobiography, *An Italian Grows in Brooklyn*, by denying a Prince Spaghetti commercial of school children running home for lunch. He said the Italians never ate lunch at home in the Gravesend section of Brooklyn.

Here in Ithaca, I never had lunch at home either. What I had every school day, between 12:00 and 1:15, was dinner.

No peanut butter and jelly sandwich for Mom's children. They were like four letter words as far as she was concerned. We had spaghetti or stuffed peppers made with eggplant, homemade prosciutto, bread, Romano cheese, tomatoes and of course olive oil and garlic. If it was Friday during Lent, we had *baccala* (codfish) or spaghetti with clam or lobster sauce or meatless pizza. I always felt sorry for my friends; their vegetables were so unimaginative. I had dandelions, spinach, broccoli or twenty other vegetables sautéed with olive oil and garlic.

\* \* \*

Whenever the air raid siren blows, it means Henry St. John Elementary schoolers have to stop whatever we are doing, grab our coats and walk home as quickly as possible. That wailing, brain-piercing sound frightens even the sun and wind. They can run and hide, close up shop. The sun by turning off its light. The wind by holding its breath.

I can't do that. I have to walk that one city block that suddenly stretches out to feel like three, all alone. I can be in a coal mine, that's how desolate, abandoned I feel. Usually there are dogs and cats and birds and an occasional car and neighbor out to fill the spaces between the houses.

Not this one particular blue-less day forever glued with white school paste to my memory cells. No pets are sunning themselves on the sidewalk, waiting for the three o'clock dismissal bell to ring. No birds call back and forth to each other, sharing information about the movement of particular squirrels or cats. The long, eerie-feeling block is totally empty, deserted. All life has ceased. I am the only human left until I reach my back door, open it and go inside, closing out the terrifying silence.

\* \* \*

It's recess, we've divided up into two teams. It's my turn at bat. I look at the pitcher, my classmate in 6th grade at Henry St. John School. She winds up, shoots a ball to me. I look at it coming toward me and freeze. If I swing at it and miss, I will feel like such a failure. A dummy. I let my team down. All that expended energy ending up in nothing. Just a swish of the bat.

Strike one.

The kids in the outfield shift from one foot to the other. Jack is on second base. He's antsy. He wants to run. He wants to score. "Come on, Jemma, bat me in." I fantasize a long high ball right over center field.

Strike two.

This is my last chance. I realize I'm gripping the bat as tight as I grip a chicken, holding down its legs and wings while Mom slits its throat. That is done in private in our cellar, no eyes on me. Out here I'm so vulnerable. Everyone is watching me. I can't bear to make a mistake.

Strike three.

# BLUE MOON

Sunday afternoons, if a movie does not fill in the hours or if it is too cold or too wet to be outside playing, my brother Fred and I escape to the blue and gray mohair couch, read the funnies and the Parade magazine section, and then I listen while he tells me everything about his two favorite subjects.

To me all cars look alike—either red roses, huge black ants, or Cinderella's coach. As each passes by our windows, Fred rhapsodizes on their make, year, model, miles per gallon, cost, designer, engine size, faults and fantasies. None ever compares to his all-time favorite, Jaguars. Those beauties are in a class by themselves and he is going to own one— after college.

Does my younger, gifted sibling ever realize that he will not be able to slip a Jag under his arm, like the head of an opponent football player, and take it to Lambaréné, Gabon, after he graduates from med school and makes his other dream come true—to work side by side with Le Grand Docteur in his African jungle hospital. Fred isn't even a teenager when he reads that Albert Schweitzer has been a world-class organist, an authority on Bach, a theologian, and a philosopher with Ph.D.s and publications in all three fields before going back to medical school and then devoting his entire life to the starving natives, many suffering from malaria, dysentery, and leprosy.

Knowing my brother as little as I do, nevertheless I'm certain he could have been capable of tenderly dismantling a Jaguar, packing it, and shipping it up the Ogowe River to Lambaréné

But the morning comes when Mom has to call a doctor. Her son cannot get out of bed. He is at Cornell University, a pre-med freshman, so what can be wrong? The heart-broken, uncomprehending look and the shame in her voice lock into my memory. Her precious treasure is ambulanced to Strong Memorial Hospital in Rochester, 90 miles away. How could the God she prayed to every morning at 7 a.m. let this happen?

Soon after, I learn that Strong Memorial is a psychiatric hospital. The handsome, six-foot champion wrestler, who once managed to pin an Olympic wrestler, is given shock treatments by the attending psychiatrists—without a thorough examination. That Mom is paying for his confinement bothers Fred so much that he signs himself out and returns home.

I see very little of my younger brother as the decades pass. He follows in Dad's and his brother's footsteps, buying income property. The proceeds allow him to periodically escape to Chile and to the Amazon, where he visits aboriginal tribes and gathers up many soul-satisfying memories.

Once again, after decades have passed, Fred and I are corresponding. Letters are now replacing the Sunday chats. He wants his two Brazilian daughters to have pictures of their father, the house in which he lived, their grandparents and aunts and uncles. I surprise and delight my brother with those memories one day. He writes that he is very content working with the homeless. I write telling him how pleased I am that the spirit of Le Grand Docteur is alive and well in Rio de Janeiro. In my next letter, I shall ask him what make of car he drives.

# IT'S NOT UNUSUAL

I had heard the talk. As a young girl I'd heard about Zia Rosalia—my Dad's sister, my aunt. I never criticized nor condemned her, but I was old enough to understand that Zia Rosalia's story brought shame, or that I *should* feel shame. But I never did.

> Shhh! Don't say that word out loud! *Che disgrazia!*

And then, as I aged and read about my culture and its institutions—and the institutions the institutions created—it seemed only natural that a dirt-floor-poor, uneducated woman who was as young and more gorgeous than Elizabeth Taylor and Katherine Hepburn combined—and a mother abandoned by her husband, who used the excuse that he was going to South America to find work—behaved as she was reported to have behaved. When I was twenty-three and visiting my relatives in Fondi, Mom's brother, Zio Vincenzo, told me he had seen Zia Rosalia in one of "those" houses. My question: what the hell was *he* doing there? But I didn't ask it then.

I met Zia Rosalia that same visit. She was living with her son, Manfredo, and his family. What impressed me and endeared Manfredo to me was his total acceptance of his mother. I wish I could have told him how pleased I was that he didn't treat his mother as other relatives did, but my Italian was not that good.

Older than Dad, Zia Rosalia had to be in her late sixties—old by my standards then! Dumpy and as wrinkled as a prune, with all her mistakes showing on her face, even she, by her gestures, registered disbelief that the dark-haired, dark-eyed young woman in the 3" x 5" picture she picked up from a dresser to show me was really she.

It doesn't happen so much any more. Maybe it is I who have changed, and not attitudes. But twenty to twenty-five years ago, I occasionally interacted with people who felt superior to me because they had letters after their names, or their husbands did, and they were usually associated with Cornell University. At the time I had neither a husband nor a profession nor stature, nor impressive letters after my name (and I still don't), but I was often involved in organizations that attracted people of such backgrounds. Many of them were lovely, generous, caring people. But when I detected that pseudo-superior, fear-with-her-hair-combed attitude in someone's voice as she started telling me about her daughter-lawyer, or her doctor-son, or her husband-executive-director, I would tell the story of Zia Rosalia.

The first time I did so, the words just started coming out of their own volition and energy. There was no premeditation, nor was there shame or embarrassment in my voice. I was just doing what others were doing: sharing family history.

But as I told my story, everyone seemed to notice how warm it was, or how cold. How lovely the forsythia was, or how vibrant the fall leaves, and had I had a chance to go for a drive to see them? I was perfectly content to change the subject and ease on down the road.

If my aunt had been a prostitute, she chose that means of supporting herself and her son from a very limited list of possibilities. Fondi was not a northern Italian factory town with opportunities for employment. It was a farm village, and Zia Rosalia was uneducated. I prefer to think of her as having been adventuresome and daring.

Many years later I learned that, in fact, my aunt supported herself by being a seamstress.

## BLOOD AND INK

A snatch
of Rosalia
between lined sheets

Back wards
muffle
us women

Sex
makes the word
go round

A writer's
whoring
gets published

A whore's
whoring
gets punished

Mom's face
casts a long shadow
on my novel

Loneliness
laps
at our sanity

Zia Lucia shuffles
through
black ink

Backwards
lose
a lot of talent

The red light district
sends shame
up and down Mom's face

I write
between
blood lines

Bed sheets
press together
in my diary

The red light
illuminates
the cultural gap

Silence
screams
across generations

Their loneliness
confuses
my imagination

Book leaves
pile up
the truth

Blood
smears
the connection

My resolve
wavers
under the red light

The pain
runs
out of ink. ~JM

 WHAT A BEAUTIFUL SIGHT AMONG THE POTS AND PANS

Mirrors come in every size, shape, and form. Looking into the ten-foot Pier glass mirror in my living room, and seeing the faces of relatives as I sit and write, I am reminded that words are mirrors – reflectors of who we are, what we are, how we are feeling or not feeling.

The Pier mirror is not original to this house; Mom bought it at a private house sale a few years before her death. Framed in gold-painted, ornately designed plaster, with an attached white marble shelf, it enhanced an already beautiful room. Only in the past decades have Pier glass mirrors grown in value, reflective of the increased respect for historic houses.

Italian-American women writers are also a rarity. In my diary entries I declare that I exist. I am a mind seeking universal truth, a heart beating in sync with as yet unknown hearts. At a subconscious level I am rebelling against a culture that demands submission. Great achievements start out small, quietly. The incubation period can take decades.

Five decades later, wanting to give voice to my silent female relatives, thus giving voice to myself as well – and wanting to find a means of expression, a mirror to distance myself even more from their experiences – I wrote and gave poetry readings about those experiences.

## LEARNING TO FLY

I am the pen, the paper,
the thoughts, the memories, the silence,
the pain, the victim.

I am the words, the calm, the peace,
the joy, the light, the forgiveness,
the compassion, the power, the transcendent,
the victor.

I am the magic, the miracle, the unexplainable,
the beginning, the end, the endless,
I AM.
~JM

# DREAM YOUR TROUBLES AWAY

When I think of Dad's sister, Zia Lucia, I can feel sad, very sad. If I choose, I am no longer a child in a world that doesn't make sense, a world in which the only way to survive was not to feel, not to ask questions for which there were no logical answers, to stuff confusion and wonder and silence deeper and deeper inside myself – and of course, become depressed like the other women in my family.

I can think about Zia Lucia and bring the understanding I have gained to this page, as white and plain and fragile as her wedding gown. Easily crumpled, like her life.

Young Irish women came here to work as maids cleaning other women's grand homes. Young Italian women came as part of a family, or to create a family. Their only identity was to be the one who kept the family together.

When Adolfo Camilli, Dad's roommate back in the '20's, shared with him his longing for a wife, Dad showed him a picture of his petite, rather pretty sister Lucia, who was left back in Fondi. Lucia allowed herself to buy a dream, and to be bought. She came to America to marry Adolfo.

Two of Lucia and Adolfo's sons were twins. She preferred the lighter-skinned one, and took him out for walks in his carriage, leaving the darker-skinned son, Johnny, home. The preferred son caught a cold or pneumonia – and died.

Zia spent the following thirty-eight years in Willard State Mental Hospital, located between Cayuga and Seneca lakes in New York. All the years her children were growing up, she was locked up. And they, my cousins, spent their childhood visiting their mother – Sundays, 2:00 – 4:00.

The number of women put away into mental institutions before, during, and after World War II is legion. Oftentimes, it was to be rid of them. But Mom said in this case, it was to help. Mom always spoke highly of Adolfo. He came to visit often. I remember him being friendly and without anger. Without melancholy.

In 1974 the doors to the back wards across the U.S. were opened. Mental patients were dumped out. Go home. Go find yourself. Make a life.

It was Johnny who took care of his mother, my aunt, in her home, until he died. She outlived three of her sons. Today, the youngest lives out west. I think I know why.

 MELODY OF LOVE

The days I remember my Dad taking time to relax, have supper with his children before going back to the hotel until closing time of one a.m., he sometimes seemed at peace, satisfied with his life. That was not the time to bring up the past. To ask how his father died. What was his mother like? Wasn't it painful to leave behind sisters and mother and friends and familiar scenes of cobblestone arches and streets and the low hills?

This definitely wasn't the time to ask him why Mom was angry or why they weren't speaking to each other. I could sense Mom had preferred to be married to a velvet-suited, French-speaking *padrone*. She wanted a car and possibly a chauffeur. Dad still had rough spots—he picked up food, fish with his hands. He preferred walking and riding the bus. Once I accompanied him on a city bus up to Cornell and back. As I looked at the storefronts and the lecture halls, I still remember wondering if I could ever find my way up there alone. It seemed so far away from my sheltered, fenced-in world. Mom must have felt that way at times.

It dawns on me this whole story is about love and the lack of it and the abundance of it. Dad expressed his love for us in his work, the income it produced and how well we lived. When I think of Mom, her love manifested in the constant procession of Italian dishes she put before us every day. With no car and the A&P three blocks away, how did she get the 25-pound bags of flour home? I have no memory of that, but I do remember the two of us carrying large brown paper bags full of heavy oranges and grapes and spinach and gallon cans of olive oil.

# I AIN'T GOT NO GRAVY FOR MY RICE

I am mute. I am a shadow. I am dust under the doormat. I do not know how I feel or how I do not feel. I have no words with which to explore that question. I do not know who I am, other than female. I watch birds; I do not soar with them. I look at mountains; I do not identify with them.

In an instant I am made sad, sexless, powerless. With one unpredicted, unplanned act, I am separated from myself. My sexual, creative, artistic, and intellectual growth are slowed. Fear, rigidity, conformity begin to ossify.

I am in pain. I cannot sit through a two-hour movie without constantly shifting to ease the ache in my tailbone. I say nothing to Mom.

In my three years in junior high school, the most significant event to occur, the event that is still influencing me, happened right at home—in the house where I still live. In the kitchen. Seemingly without warning—on a sunny day—my sad, lonely, angry mother kicked me. There is absolutely no memory of why it happened, or what I did or said, or didn't say or do, to provoke such an act. There is also no memory of my reaction. Only the resulting pain. The physical pain never healed, and my compacted nervous system grew more and more dysfunctional over the decades.

So my chiropractor, Dr Pierre Gremaud, was correct when he identified the injury to my coccyx as being at least 35 years old.

After a few adjustments from him, the back pain ceased. Not only that, but over the following years of adjustments—though I tell my friends and disbelievers that this makes no sense intellectually, even to me—I experienced improved night vision, lack of dizziness while dancing, diminished motion sickness when traveling, and more energy.

I also experienced total healing of mastitis in my right breast.

Whenever I released the traumas that surfaced from my subconscious, however, I experienced great pain throughout my body. The pain and the mental images of various life experiences informed me of the damage I was releasing from body tissue and cell memory. Even if the brain forgets, the cells remember trauma, and as cells become involved in healing they release those old memories to the conscious mind again. As that happens, the body releases the energy that was being used by the negative experiences, and it can then be better used toward the rejuvenation of cells, organs, and body functions.

As Deepak Chopra M.D. asks in his book *Quantum Healing*, why are we still ill, when our cells are constantly renewing themselves?

* * *

I learn to watch my step around my mother. How can a hand on my teenage breast feel so delicious? Where do those never-experienced feelings of such pleasure come from? Feelings so strong, I am ambivalent about whether to stay on my mother's lap, though I know that what is happening is wrong.

Hearing the kitchen door open and close and my older brother's footsteps cross the floor, in a moment he will come into the living room and see me on my mother's lap. That thought causes my face muscles to constrict. I can feel the shame and embarrassment rise in me, causing me to pull Mom's hand out from the front of my dress so that I can get away before we are seen. I wonder in that brief moment why her actions don't seem to bother her.

Who is this woman I call my mother? Why does she behave so strangely and awfully? How I wish I could live somewhere else. Why doesn't she go back to Italy? She talks about doing so whenever she is angry. Or why doesn't Dad leave? Then I could go with him and get away from her.

* * *

It is another ordinary day in my childhood, a few years before my mother will kick me. I am a mute observer, for the only time, to what was not an uncommon occurrence for my sister Mary.

In the kitchen, just home from school, I may have been having a glass of fresh-squeezed lemonade and perhaps some home-canned pears or an oatmeal cookie from the batch Mary had made the day before. Mom is there with me.

The door from outside into the kitchen opens very, very carefully. Through the pane of glass I see my petite, beautiful, shiny-black-wavy-haired sister home from high school. She doesn't open the door wide and hurry in, eager to drop her books and share her day with us. Instead, she peeks in carefully and just enough to be able to look around, her eyes darting around the room. When she sees Mom, her body tightens, her eyes darken. I sense some kind of shield go up around her as she hesitates and then silently enters the room, closing the door very carefully.

Immediately, in Italian, Mom accuses her of being late, of having stopped to talk to some boys, of being lazy. To this day I wonder where Mary found the wisdom to not respond. The curtain descends; that's all I can remember.

Now I understand the role my sister played in protecting me from our mother's sudden acts of suppressed rage. And I comprehend how I protected my younger brother Fred until I left when he was fourteen.

# A FINE ROMANCE

Let's say it was at a football game that I met the man I married and lived with for eleven years. If it's not true, it's close. My marriage very much resembled a football game. I lost every game every year, but won the pennant. Fear, brute force, arbitrary rules, uniforms, alcohol, elimination of the weak, half-time celebrations, bruises, aches, pains of the heart and soul, and that goal line always being beyond my reach.

The pre-game show was impressive. When I told Mom the name of the boy who had invited me to the movies, she was thrilled. She saw him every Sunday, escorting his father and nearly blind mother to 7:00 a.m. mass. Such a fine son! He spent his days working in his father's music store. A good provider for her daughter and grandchildren. His father was at mass every morning, with my mother and a few other unhappy people. *Che bella famiglia.* I didn't have a chance.

# WITHOUT A SONG

Why does everything have to be so painful? Should I marry? Should I give him back the solitaire? Will anyone else ever love me? Is it just that I'm new at all this, and things will calm down after the ceremony? They say all brides are nervous before the wedding. Isn't there somebody who can help me get out of this?

This is normal. Just stay calm and pray; everything will work out. It rained yesterday; is that a good sign or a bad sign. When I tell my fiancé Tom about my doubts, he tells me he'll beat me if I change my mind.

Dad can tell I am unhappy. Why doesn't he do something to stop the wedding? I know he's awfully sick, but surely he could tell Tom I've changed my plans and to please go away.

Oh, you're just being normal. It's only a few more days and then everything will be okay.

Back and forth, over and over, all these thoughts—and more—parade and swirl and run through my mind. My brother Jim notices how unhappy I look, and he tries to get me to cancel the wedding. But I can't listen to him. *Jim isn't going to boss me around like Mom tried to make me believe he has the right to!*

I wanted to go to college like my brothers. But Mom told me that for girls, it was marriage or the convent.

I am so confused I go to bed and stay there for a few days. And still the wedding plans continue. My bridesmaids are chosen. Mom orders the flowers for the church. My gown arrives in a huge box full of tissue paper. I take it out and hang it up to keep it from wrinkling. The showers with the nightgowns, toasters, sheets and towels come and go. We turn the dining room into a display room for all the gifts. How many toasters or wine carafes or sheets and towel sets does a family use in one lifetime?

Looking over all the wedding presents as they start coming, I wonder if they will outlast the marriage.

My favorite gift is from Mom and Dad. It is a six-place setting of sterling silver with a lily-of-the-valley pattern. Like the ones that grow in the garden around the house.

## LA BELLA FIGURA, Part 2

Saturday, August 22, 1953, two months after my high school graduation, I wake up early, nervous, excited, scared, depressed, anticipating, hopeful, uncertain. It is sunny and warm—a good omen, I pray. Mom fixes me the same breakfast I have had every morning for as long as I can remember, including a raw egg drunk out of the shell and fresh-squeezed orange juice.

Eventually I begin to dress, putting on appropriate underwear and the full-length slip trimmed in lace. As I look at my dress, the satin and lace and the beads around the V-neck, I remember the day in Rochester when I agreed with Mom to buy it. I don't especially like it, but I am not accustomed to having my way where she is concerned.

It doesn't matter.

Oh, how I would much rather be dressing for another graduation. To be putting on a cap and gown in preparation for marching down the aisle of an auditorium with my senior class. To be getting a B.S. after my name rather than an Mrs. before a name that isn't even mine. But I threw that dream over the Stewart Avenue bridge, where local college students often go to commit suicide.

This is really Mom's day, anyway. She chose the music, the singers, the three-priest Mass, the five-tiered cake, the dinner, the reception food, the band, the hall, the photographer, the guest list of 800, and the husband.

 THE BEAT GOES ON

So what was I going to do with my life after I married? Did I have a life? Where would we live? Where would I live while Tom fulfilled his military obligation? To answer those questions meant I had to have a history of asking questions and expecting reasonable answers.

The thought of being alone in an apartment upset me so much, I stopped looking after seeing one or two. It didn't occur to me to get a job or take some courses. What this frightened newlywed decided was to live at home. With the Korean War over, Tom was sent to Fort Dix in New Jersey to fulfill his military obligation. I spent my days helping Mom carry home grocery bags full of broccoli and oranges, meat and fish; hanging up white shirts and sheets on the line, colored socks and pants on another. Tuesday I ironed, Fridays I cleaned.

After the six weeks of boot camp, Tom was given weekend leaves. On Saturday evenings we would have dinner with his parents; then he'd take me out to the Royal Palm bar, a short walk from his parents' home. Royal Palm--another of those crazy-named bars owned by another Italian family. The bar was in Collegetown, the shopping, eating and drinking section of Cornell University, in the city with the second least amount of sun in the nation. The bar's only windows faced the street, leaving the two long rooms dark. Not my choice of how to spend my time. We sat in a booth, separate from the bar. I would sip on a coke or root beer, Tom would order a Genny beer—and another, and another. Before we married, we fed the jukebox and jitterbugged. After the marriage he told me that I no longer knew how to dance.

One Saturday night my feelings about not being happy with the way I was spending my time took over. My coke went flat, so did the conversation. Time to go home, even if I had to do it on my own. The walk was all down hill, a mile and a half maybe. Just as I was crossing Green and Geneva Street, Tom pulled up, parked in front of the house, got out of the car and hit me. "How dare you leave me? Who do you think you are going off without telling me?

But then the army sent Tom to France, and I moved back in with my parents, to what I still thought of as home.

\* \* \*

Hurricane Hazel, blowing through Ithaca on October 15, 1954, brought excitement and wonder into this teenager's life. Standing out on the front porch, I was amazed at how warm the wind was. Looking across the street, I saw century-old elm trees toppling over. It was as though a giant walked around pulling up trees like toothpicks and laying them down on top of electrical and phone lines. With outside communication cut off, there was no way for me to call an ambulance or taxi should my first child decide to be born on his due date.

Everything was so interesting, and not knowing what to expect, I wasn't concerned. Mom kept telling me not to worry.

"Don't worry, I'll go out and find someone to take you to the hospital."

"Don't worry, I'm praying for help."

"Don't worry, everything will be okay."

My son was born 5:45 a.m. on October 19th 1954. I distinctly remember thinking, as I walked into the delivery room, that my life was going to be incredibly different from that day forward. No longer would I be responsible solely for myself. Even though I was so young and unprepared, I felt the stirrings of desire to raise my children differently from the way I was raised. "The exact opposite," is how I phrased it – except for the food.

Dr. Edward Hall was the obstetrician on call that night. I remember him coming in to where I was waiting for my time and commenting on how quiet I was.

"There's no need to cry," I responded. And, indeed that was true. The delivery went well, because I was drugged to feel no pain. Back then, in the 50s, new mothers stayed in the hospital for five days. We saw our babies at feeding time; our relatives during visiting hours. The remainder of the time we rested. There were no TVs and no phones in the room. Just hope that the future would be as easy as the delivery. My brother-in-law brought us home and I added a new identity—mother—to my other ones, uncertain and poorly formed as they were.

"Where did you learn to take care of a baby?" I recall Mom asking me as she watched me bathe, dress and feed him; then take her grandson out for walks in the late fall and winter sunshine.

*  *  *

I wish my father had felt the same. Something was going wrong and until very recently, I never knew exactly why. The person who had on occasions defended me and protected me, was suddenly angry that I was living in his home. Dad was very ill at the time; high blood pressure and nephritis had forced him to retire. He rented out the hotel and, now as I think about it, his idleness may have made him more unhappy and nervous. Maybe that's why he became upset over a phone bill of a few long distance calls. The man who, a year earlier, had paid thousands of dollars for a wedding and then had given me $500 to open a savings account in my name, was angry because I hadn't offered to pay for my calls. It didn't make sense. I felt like an unwanted stranger in someone else's house. After that our relationship was never the same. Even though he was certain that I now paid my expenses, Dad nevertheless stopped speaking to me. Where was I to go? What was I to do differently?

I'm not sure who came up with an idea that turned into a solution: why didn't I go to France with my infant son and join my husband! Was it Mom's idea? My mother-in-law's? The two of them together? I'll never know, but I bless them anyway.

Somehow Father William Byrne, our pastor, became involved. He presented me with some leftover travelers checks from a recent trip. Golly, I was actually going to do some traveling. Get to see a foreign country. Better yet, live in one for six months. A mostly unexplored dream was coming true. How incredibly wonderful!

But how would I feed my baby? Did they have baby food? Was the water safe? What would I do for a crib? How difficult would it be traveling with an infant with no one to help me? Supposing he became ill? Or me? Would we have central heating?

In the time it took to apply and receive my passport, make Lehigh Valley train arrangements to New York City and plane arrangements from Idlewild airport (now called JFK) to Paris, I learned that people and children manage to live and breathe in Europe as they do here. Somehow we would be fine. I bet my eyes rivaled the stars, I was so excited.

Trans World Airlines. Isn't that a beautiful name? Don't you just love the images it conjures up! A big bird was going to take the two of us into its belly and transport us, effortlessly, to the Land of Oz. This Oz had the Eiffel Tower and the Louvre Museum and the river Seine. The hotel in Paris, where the three of us stayed for a few days, arranged a babysitter for me so that I actually saw the Mona Lisa, the famous Winged Victory of Samothrace, and countless other priceless art treasures. Thrilled to actually be standing in front of Leonardo Da Vinci's famous painting, I made a move to get close enough to touch it. The guard was familiar with tourists like me and so I had to be content just looking at that smile.

From Paris, a train ride southwest to Bordeaux allowed me to see more of the French countryside. In Bordeaux, we were instructed to catch a bus outside the Globe Hotel that would take us to a little fishing village called Andernos-Les-Bains. It is situated on a sheltered cove of the Atlantic, called le Bassin d'Arcachon. Madame Perreaud, our landlady, told us that the tide goes out five miles – or maybe it was five kilometers – every day.

My three years of high school French were coming in handy. Germaine Perreaud was a World War II widow. Her husband, a civilian who supplied food to the military, was accidentally shot and killed and Mamma, as she instructed me to call her, still mourned his absence and wore black, ten years later.

Villa Ric Rac on Avenue Pasteur was charming. Perfect. For extra income, Mamma had divided her house in half, furnishing it extremely nicely with French pieces I wished I could take home with me. The kitchen was huge, with a red tile floor and a coal stove for heating and cooking. The house was one of the more modern ones in the village, with central heating and an indoor bathroom complete with bidet and tub. The only addition we made was to somehow obtain a refrigerator.

\* \* \*

Though Tom was a corporal in the army, he was stationed at the Bordeaux Air Force Base somewhere nearby. By his orders, I was not allowed to set foot on the base, so I have no idea where it was. Whatever I needed, he bought.

I may have been born with a silver spoon in my mouth, but my hands must have been holding a dust mop. Keeping house is what I'm good for. If only I could be content cleaning toilets, I would be so happy. There's no doubt about what is clean and what isn't.

Army life starts in the middle of the night. Tom was gone before sunrise every morning, and that gave me ample time to put a smile back on my face and enjoy the rare opportunity to live in another country. Fred was an easy-going, happy child who seldom cried. He played with his toys in a playpen of sorts I made from lashing two chairs together, padding them with blankets and strapping him in so he wouldn't fall. He spent after-breakfast hours in that manner while I hand-washed the previous days' diapers and clothes, mopped the red-tiled kitchen floor and performed other household tasks, which during the cold months included feeding the furnace.

Andernos had such mild winters, getting out for walks and visits with Mamma's friends were never a problem; it was a joy. Spring arrived about a month after I did, and the beach was a couple of blocks away. When summer showed up, Fred played with the sand while I watched the tide, either coming in or going out. I know the mesmerizing motion of the waves served to calm me down from whatever disturbed me. How sad that Tom was unable to appreciate his son. He saw Fred as an intrusion, something unpleasant to have around. To pick him up and hold him was alien to him.

When I ask him to play with his son, he'd just say "come on," in a tone suggesting ridiculousness on my part.

Mamma made everything all right. She was a friend, a mother, an equal, a superior. I loved her, and I often thought of naming a daughter after her. Germaine. Isn't that a beautiful name? Living in a country where woman's work never ended, she devised a variation on the menage-a-trois theme that worked well. Isidor and Roza were bachelor brothers; they needed meals cooked and laundry washed, while Mamma needed wood chopped for the cook stove, the garden tended, and occasional male strength for other tasks. Isidor was the thin, more reserved one. Roza, whose real name was Edmundo but who answered to a shortened version of the their last name, Rozazza, was a bit more friendly and, portly, shall we say. Occasionally I was invited to join in on after-dinner conversations. Since they were born in Italy, I loved hearing about their childhood. They were my historical novels, my adventure stories.

When Mamma suggested a visit to Lourdes, where the Virgin Mary had appeared to three young children, Tom and I accepted her offer of caring for Fred and off we went for the weekend. I came away from the experience with a third crack in my belief system. The first two came when I was growing up. I didn't like the taste of the communion wafer, and the smell of the oil used in the sacrament of Confirmation bothered me. In Lourdes, the streets of souvenir shops that fanned out from the Basilica like spokes in a wheel puzzled and offended me. Were we believers, there to experience holiness, or just to buy a plaster Madonna? I felt no sense of holiness there, but, given the number of abandoned crutches nailed to a wall, others must have. Wanting to gift Mamma for her kindness, I succumbed to a plaster Madonna only to have it rejected. Mamma was still angry at God for taking her much-loved husband from her. Thinking back on that experience, putting it together with many others in later years that resulted in my eventually leaving that belief system, perhaps I did have a whole-ly experience at Lourdes after all.

# AFTER THE BALL IS OVER

One morning I woke up and the party was over. The bell had tolled for me. No more almond or chocolate croissants. No more thinking in French, walks along the beach, or digging for clams when the tide is out. They all became memories, placed in my suitcase with my clothes. My handkerchief became soggy, hugs and kisses made the rounds, over and over. Promises to write were heard across the land. The heart responded. Would I ever see Mamma again? That was too painful a question, so I focused my attention on my ten-month-old son, who was eager to walk.

Keeping Fred confined to my lap on the plane was not possible. He spent a joy-filled time in the aisle, walking from seat to seat, showing the passengers his toys and his 4-tooth smile. When we spoke, he mimicked me, saying "Mamma" with the French accent.

Back in Ithaca, back with Mom and Dad while I waited for Tom to be discharged, my one consuming thought was to leave my husband. How could I stay with a man who continued to physically mistreat me; who refused to help with some of my heavy carry-on luggage or 30-pound Fred, who treated his son like garbage? I saw no exit signs or U-turns. Catholics don't divorce. There's no such thing as remarriage if you're not wearing black. Who would be a father to my son? I wanted more children. Where would I live if I left him? How would I support myself? But life with Mom would be an even worse fate.

Three cracks in one's belief system did not add up to freedom. I felt the jaws of the church clamp shut, but the thoughts never left me in peace.

Of course I was making all my decisions based on fear. But that was the currency of the realm. That's what I breathed in with my mother's milk, with being female, Catholic, already with the responsibility of wanting to raise a happy, well-adjusted child. The courage to end my unhappy marriage never came directly to me, but eventually someone opened the door. I hesitantly peeked in, became accustomed to what I saw and ended up eternally grateful for the assistance.

\* \* \*

Tom's commitment to Uncle Sam ended and we found an apartment. He went back to work with his father and brother-in-law at the family music store. Wednesday night dinner conversation with his parents focused on home buying. "I will give you the down payment. Don't waste your money on rent. When your mother and I married, I brought her home to this house." My choice of father-in-law as provider far outdistanced my choice of a husband. That reality would become even more evident in future years.

A few months later we moved into our three-bedroom, Cape Cod style home with almost an acre of yard. It was just outside of Ithaca, a mile and a half from downtown. The mortgage was forever—25-years— and the monthly payment was $83.38. Maybe things will be better.

\* \* \*

Dad died May 5, 1956. I was pregnant with my second child. Those memories are still in Technicolor.

He had stopped working four years before his death. High blood pressure and nephritis was the diagnosis. It wasn't the work that wore away at his vigor; it was the unhappiness. The hotel was rented out. Someone told me he occasionally played cards down at the Sons of Italy, which was a few blocks away from our house. If only he had left Mom, like I so often wished he had. I would have gone with him and kept house for him.

But our relationship never reverted back to the way it was before I married. When I returned from France, in August of 1955, naturally I stayed with Dad and Mom until my husband returned and we found an apartment while we went house-hunting. Dad was still angry with me, so conversation was non-existent, but he did enjoy his grandson. Especially when Fred III was about a year old and would run to get his grand-dad an ashtray if he saw him pull out a cigarette and light it.

What took Dad to the emergency room the night of May 4th, 1956, was a heart attack. I chose to stay with Mary's two children and mine while she and Mom were at the hospital. Since Dad no longer wanted to see me, I felt the best way I could show my love was to stay away. How I longed to be with him. To see what was going on; how he was being treated. But there was nothing to say to him and everything to say to him.

It was I who called Mom the next morning to ask about Dad's condition. He had died during the night but, because I was pregnant, she didn't want to tell me.

I don't remember crying. What I clearly recall is how glad I felt that he was finally free of all those years of unhappiness. Back then, in the Italian culture, death was the only exit. Contracts were written in stone. Finally he was free from my mother. I was happy for him for that.

I believed in heaven and hell and purgatory then, and was told Dad had seen a priest and made a confession. So I was pleased that he was in purgatory making up for his sins and that I would one day see him again. Of that I had no doubts. Whenever Mom accused him of having a girlfriend, I wished it were true; that it was one of his sins.

True to Italian custom, the wake was at home in our double living rooms. Naturally he was dressed in his blue suit. Naturally Mom bought an expensive casket.

The flowers were lovely. The first person to pay his respects was a black man. That pleased me. Mom had never seen such dark-skinned people until she came to Ithaca. She was always frightened of them and tried to instill that fear in me. Dad felt otherwise.

Of course, all the *paesani* came, sat and stayed. The wake was at least two days. Somehow I had to convey to my father how much he meant to me. It was too late for words so I told him by kneeling by the casket and holding and stroking his hand. Eventually someone lifted me away and the casket was closed. Being the youngest female, I was once again relegated to the end of the line in church. First my mother, then my brothers and sister, then me.

Dad is not in the casket or in the ground. He is with me. I never go to the cemetery to "visit" him; there is no need.

\* \* \*

Early on Halloween morning, October 31, 1956, Shannon was born. How happy I was to have a daughter. Tom had insisted that his son carry on the family name, so he was Frederick Thomas Wilcox III. My turn came with our second child. Somewhere I had heard the name, Shannon, and simply loved it. Often I would consider Italian names like Mario or Benamino or Filomina, and wonder why I couldn't give my children Italian names.

When our third child, a second son, was born in January 1962, I asked my husband "Do you like the name A. Lincoln Wilcox?" (I had always loved Abraham Lincoln, but it was many years before I learned why.)

"No, I don't." he responded, but offered no alternative. Neither did he ridicule my preference or tease me, this time. As usual, I caved in, and came up with another name, Jay Joseph, which I didn't like – but Tom did. So I accepted it.

1962 was an interesting year. John Kennedy was in the White House; South Viet Nam was in the news. So was the rigging of TV programs. Charles Van Doren was found guilty of perjury charges. "Lucky" Luciano, head of the U.S. Mafia, died on January 26th. My third child was born into a generation that was to become more and more dishonest and violent while at the same time attempting to address iniquities that have existed for centuries. And my marriage was deteriorating.

But a fourth child, our son Kelly, was born in September 1963. Naïve that I was, my thoughts about parenting ran something like this: If only I could have intelligent children, my problems in raising them would be few. Being very bright, they would automatically know to be kind, honest, helpful, hardworking, cheerful, and to study so they would do well in school and in college. They would have satisfying jobs and marriages. We would all live happily ever after.

What can you expect of a teenage mom? As I think back over the years, Tom drinking more and more, my growing loneliness and exhaustion, the arguments with Jay over mealtime and clean clothes and bedtime, were there any moments of great joy? Probably, but I don't recall any – even now.

# STORMY WEATHER

When my dearly beloved asked to borrow a suitcase so he could leave me – seemingly out of the blue – and Kelly wasn't even one year old yet, why didn't I "shimmy and shake like my sister Kate"? Instead of feeling abandoned, confused, helpless, like being thrown into the lake with my arms tied behind my back, I could have packed up the four kids, ten dozen cloth diapers, baseball bats and Barbie dolls, given the three cats away, flown to Nevada, and made over $100,000 a year in one of those "houses." In a couple years, I could have returned, bought a home up on East Hill and lived happily ever after.

What still fascinates me is that the pen picked me up the day Tom left, and together we started recording my existence. With absolutely no understanding of the healing properties of sound, I sang, or maybe hummed, for three days before collapsing on the couch, wondering how all this could be happening to me. The understanding that it was I who left him would come later – all I could think about then was how to feed and shelter my children and send them to college.

It was Labor Day, 1964. Nine-year-old Fred and seven-year-old Shannon were outside, with their neighborhood friends, enjoying the last days of summer vacation. Two-and-one-half-year-old Jay and infant Kelly ate, played, or napped, as usual.

The civil war that had raged on and on inside of me for eleven years was almost over. Reconstruction had begun. It, too, would be long and painful, tearing my family apart in agonizing ways I could never have imagined. But as weeks went by, I began noticing how nice it was without the children's father. No complaints about how I expected him to come home after work and have dinner with us. Then I began noticing how wonderful it was without Tom. No complaints about how noisy the children are. Then I noticed how great it was without my husband. No complaints about me being a nag because I suggested he hold his youngest child or talk to him.

Two other more significant changes were that Shannon's morning stomach aches ceased, and the twice-monthly trips to the pediatrician and drugstore ended. For the past six months Jay and Kelly had been passing respiratory infections back and forth.

## GETTING AWAY WITH MURDER

He beat her up.
She smiled and forgave him.
He raped her.
She didn't know there was anything she could do.

He abandoned her.
She had a nervous breakdown.
He refused to support them.
She went into therapy.
He tried to turn the children against her.
She went to school.
He drank more.
She graduated magna cum laude.
He developed a brain tumor.
Her stories appeared in literary magazines.
They said the alcohol killed him before the cancer.
She knew better.

~JM

# THE VIEW FROM THE BRIDGE

Climb up He said
So she did
Perching herself on the crossbeam
What do you see? He asked. A lemming-like mass of humanity.
He pulled out her nails.
She climbed down.
They went for a
Walk together. ~JM

My three-priest, five-bridesmaids, 800-guest marriage occurred in 1953 when I was eighteen. The un-marrying, with two attorneys, took two years, 1964 and 1965.

What a blessing that was. Without enough formal education, the only jobs available to me would have me at tasks I couldn't handle. My damaged spine made most types of repetitive labor impossible. I was also quite depressed, and caring for my children and the problems that surfaced were beginning to overwhelm me. What little I could earn would be eaten up by childcare, or transportation expenses, or other surprises.

*If you don't know how to choose a good husband, at least pick a peach of a father-in-law.*

\* \* \*

Frederick Thomas Wilcox Sr. was a few inches shorter than his six-foot-tall son. What was left of his hair was dark, but his eyes, behind glasses, had a bright, positive glow to them, especially when he conversed with me. He was slim, no sagging belly, a very healthy looking man. Someone I was proud to have as family.

He attended mass every morning and then worked in his music store every day except Sunday. Every night after dinner he read the paper, smoked a cigar, kissed his wife, Irene, good-night and went to bed around eight.

The day after Tom left, my father-in-law paid the electric bill so the service could be turned back on. A few months later he paid the doctor and hospital bills for my hernia surgery.

In effect, I became my father-in-law's employee. The self-written job description was to raise his grandchildren to be healthy, educated, emotionally mature, contributing members of society. In other words: how naive can one be!


*Finalmente!* After eleven years of wanting to leave my husband, but feeling caught in a trap with no release save death, after eleven years of cleaning up the nightly beer bottles, not allowed to drive, discouraged from any self-improvement activities, and blamed when he was late to work, I had my wish. But what was I going to do with the rest of my life? I didn't know how to support myself. And who would love me?

Moving back home with Mom would be like going from the frying pan to the fire. I was a very good cook—my pizza was better than any restaurant's—but something was wrong with my lower back, causing me to spend most afternoons on the couch. That meant I couldn't follow in Dad's footsteps and open a pizza parlor. Turning the care of my children over to another while I tried working for minimum wages was not an idea I could fathom. They would again feel rejected, and the quality of their care would deteriorate even more.

In her own odd way, my mother-in-law, Irene Driscoll Wilcox, was also very "helpful." Legally blind, she spent her afternoons on the phone, dishing the dirt with the girls, her evenings directly in front of the boob tube, a quart of beer and a tall glass on the rug beside her. That I was her only daughter-in-law did not make me her favorite. "Who in their right mind would name a child after a river fer Chrissake! And Shannon isn't even a saint's name." She didn't approve of her husband's decisions to support the grandchildren, and her son could do no wrong.

Irene was 67 when she died of cancer, February 17th of the following year. Her son and I were still disagreeing about child support. He was their father. They had the inherent birthright to be properly cared for. That takes money. Tom felt his salary could not be stretched that far. And besides—what he really wanted was that life would be so difficult for me I would take him back. He hinted at that at his mother's wake and, though I had finally stopped the car from rolling over me, I was not yet firmly planted in the driver's seat, road map in my head, clear, straight, dry road ahead. Yes, I was pushed and shoved out of the backseat, and I often looked at the dashboard and keys and gas pedal, but I was too frightened and confused to turn on the engine. More help was needed.

## HOW YOU GONNA KEEP 'EM DOWN ON THE FARM AFTER THEY'VE SEEN PAREE?

Bringing Father Richard Tormey into the act was like asking Al Capone to console a woman made a widow by the Corleone family. But my attorney was too old and as comforting as an icicle. Even though I knew Tom's attorney, a legal minefield separated us.

Richard Tormey wore his collar backwards but I found him handsome, smooth as silk, intellectually enriching. Being emotionally and intellectually starved, I was bowled over by his sincere desire to be of any help in finding some pot of holy Catholic glue to mend the fractured fairytale. What I had before me was the mirage of a feast, and all I was allowed to taste was a small dish of oatmeal.

There were so many questions pouring out of me. What was I to do? Should I take him back for the sake of the children? Will he change? What does God want? The Church says I can never remarry as long as he lives. Can I go out on a date? How unfair that the children will never have a father to read to them or dry their tears. I saw those questions as opportunities to call Father Tormey, either at his office in Anabel Taylor Hall at Cornell University, where he was chaplain, or at the rectory on Stewart Avenue. I wanted to call him ten times a day and every evening.

One day he invited me to lunch to discuss my questions. A beautician friend did my hair; I wore a new dress and remember being told how nice I looked.

Of course I had to repay him – which meant I could see him again. At the end of my dinner party for him, he said he couldn't remember when he'd eaten a more delicious meal, rectory food being what it was.

The table was set with a white damask cloth and napkins, Fostoria wine glasses and my sterling silver. The first course was spaghetti with meatballs and sausage. Then I served Chicken Mary with rice, sautéed broccoli, a tossed salad, Italian bread, butter, black olives, and wine. Dessert was a peach cobbler with ice cream and coffee – to stir up more conversation.

Another perfectly legitimate way to see him was to attend Sunday Mass in the chapel at Anabel Taylor Hall. Feeling as nervous as I did at seven when I received my First Communion, nevertheless I sat way up front so I could watch his every move – turning pages, blessing us, preaching his sermon. I wondered if he noticed my hats. They were magical, wide brimmed hats that took the sadness from my eyes, turned up the corners of my mouth, transformed me into someone else for an hour a week.

During my marriage I had read historical romances; before that, movies with Jean Tierney, Ava Gardner, and Ingrid Bergman filled this teenage brain with fantasies. How I longed to have Father Tormey sing to me, some night in the hallway, "Josephina, please no-lean-a on da bell. When you smooch please don't pusha da bell." For Christmas I bought him a pair of gloves; he sent me a gloxinia plant. On my behalf he talked to Tom, to my father-in-law, to both attorneys, and to my sister-in-law, Barb. When he asked me if I wanted a reconciliation, I said no. After experiencing his help, attention, concern, I had something on which to base my decision. Plain Catholic glue was no longer acceptable. I still didn't know who I was, what I could do or not do, how I would live the rest of my life, or if I would have a life. I had been shown a tiny bit of Paris—there was no way I could go back to the farm.

# BEFORE THE PARADE PASSES BY

The pictures of Muslim women in their tent-like clothing covering their faces, hair, and bodies, were constantly shown on TV, along with views of the smoldering World Trade Center. The world-changing events of September 11, 2001, acted like bells ringing in my memory, awakening a long-forgotten act of emancipation.

The year is 1967. I have been divorced for a short time, thirty-two years old, still attending Sunday mass. But there are many changes occurring. In the past three years I have been reading nonfiction, mostly theology and philosophy: De Chardin, Father John Courtney Murray, Gregory Baum, to name just a few. Much of what I read I don't understand, but that's okay. I eventually learn enough to know that I no longer want to be a member of the Catholic Church. But before I leave it, forever, I stage a one-woman act of rebellion that makes me very proud of the face I see in the mirror.

Hats. Wide brimmed, with feathers, ribbons and bows. With or without veils. In colors matching or contrasting with my coat. Doesn't matter, I love them all. Besides, I feel I look better in a hat than without one. Somehow they brighten my eyes, change my looks. They give me a little height—in more ways than one.

However, by 1967 I am examining the controls our society and its institutions have over us, controls usually enforced by fear and punishment. Behave in a certain way or you will be fined, imprisoned, denied burial, communion, heaven.

Then I read that we women have to wear hats to mass to cover our hair so that men aren't distracted by it. How ridiculous. Sometimes the hats are more distracting than the hair. If men allow themselves to be disturbed, that's their problem, not mine. Who are they to inflict punishment on me for such a stupid reason?

Oh! How can I give up something I love so much—hats—to gain something I love even more? All my beautiful hats! The winter navy blue one and the wide-brimmed straw summer one, and the black one with the bow, and, and, and. How can I live without them? They are a part of me, like my arms and legs.

The Sunday morning arrived when I said, "This is it. No more hats." But what will people think of me? What will they say? I remember reading stories about how women and children in small towns were ostracized if they didn't conform to social norms. A woman's neighbors and friends shunned her. Her children were mistreated in school. If the husband had a business, it was boycotted. Walking bareheaded up the aisle to my pew, I felt naked and certain all eyes were on me.

But I did it.

And you know what? No one seemed to notice.

\* \* \*

All the years of marriage, my sister-in-law Barb and her husband, Bob, never came to any celebrations such as baptisms or birthdays. There was no mutual admiration society between the brothers-in-law, even though they both worked side by side in Fred Senior's store. So you can imagine how greatly surprised I was when Barb started calling to ask how I was. Did I need anything? How were the children taking the separation? To my further shock and joy, she did not criticize or blame me. Although I fully expected her to side with her mother, Barb did exactly the opposite. She bought Christmas gifts for the children when she discovered her brother wasn't going to. She also pumped me full of sunshine whenever I weakened into thinking I should attempt a reconciliation.

"He says he'll be different."

"How many times have you heard that, Jemma? Is he any different now?"

"No," I responded, my voice dropping an octave.

Barb's brother-in-law was a priest; Barb had seven children and would have accepted seven more. Yet there she was, supporting me. We spent hours on the phone, something I was not accustomed to doing, but I so appreciated her support. She did not find me unreasonable or demanding or rigid or selfish. She agreed that the children had an inherent right to a safe, secure, nourishing life.

It was during one of these afternoon part-therapy, part-gab sessions that I learned about Tom's "other woman." My spontaneous response was pity; not the anger, jealousy, revenge or bitterness played out in the movies and novels I consumed.

Raised as I was, in a religious box with a tight-fitting lid, I had no knowledge of the Buddhist philosophy about blessing your enemies because they enable you to grow. But now I know that Linda, the Other Woman, wasn't an enemy, she was a gift. She was helping me do what I hadn't the courage to do on my own—pull apart my emotional arrangement with the father of my children. I felt so sorry for Linda that Barb had a tough time talking me out of writing to her to explain why Tom would never help with any household chores or come home right after work or even have money for anything other than cars or beer. And she would never see him holding a child, or hear him reason in straight lines. Barb gently and consistently told me Linda was a grown woman, and wouldn't listen to me. It wasn't my responsibility to save or educate her. She would learn or not learn, the same way I did. The same way we all do – painfully. And, besides, maybe those things weren't important to her.

Of course money was always a major topic: Was Tom sending the grocery money? Yes, he was. And I told her about the $2.00 a day I earned baby-sitting. I even washed the diapers because the parents were good friends of mine; Ellen was working to put Don through college.

Mom was also sending up weekly care-packages of fresh eggs and homemade macaroni and holiday pastries and clothes for the children. My friends gave me rides to the grocery store, to bridge club, and other events.

Spring is the season of new beginnings, endless opportunities for growth, blossoming. Of course, for any of that to happen, other things had to end. Sometimes legally. The day finally came when Barb called me to tell me Pop-Pop, as my father-in-law was affectionately called, was going to mail me a weekly check to make the above all possible. He said, "Jemma and the kids will never want for anything." Barb told me to make up a budget of what I felt was needed to care for the children and the house. As it was, Pop-Pop had already been making the $83.38 monthly mortgage payment for years in lieu of a pay raise for his son.

When I asked Barb if I had the right to include expenses for the maintenance of a car (as Father Tormey urged me to do, telling me that, considering where I lived, I couldn't walk to buy groceries for the children or walk to mass or doctors' appointments), she agreed. Barb urged me to include everything I felt necessary so that the separation could become legal and the children and I could get on with our lives.

Tom was furious. He interpreted his father's generosity as interference. I agreed, in part, because Tom would never grow up if his father let him off the hook. But that was no longer my concern. I had just accepted the position of raising Pop-Pop's grandchildren. And even though I had no idea of how difficult it would be, I was eager to begin. After the separation papers were signed, Pop-Pop paid my attorney, although he and Barb and I did most of the negotiating. Soon after that Tom went to Mexico for a divorce and remarried.

But then, in 1971, my father-in-law's store was in financial trouble. Pop-Pop could no longer send me checks. He died in March.

\* \* \*

When my parents arrived in Ithaca in October of 1929, they brought with them a commitment to achievement and the willingness to work, as did most immigrants. From my father I learned that it's not how much money you have, but what you do with it that matters. I began examining my spending habits, eliminated what I decided was not important or necessary, making substitution. Instead of feeling deprived, poor and sad, I began to feel just the opposite.

Who am I? I asked. Was I valuable because I was dressed in velvet as a baby, sent to the dressmaker at twelve, given a fur coat I didn't like at fifteen? Surely my worth didn't stem from my home address or the size and cost of my car. Should I buy what I needed, or what society convinced me I couldn't live without?

The more I eliminated, the less encumbered I felt and the prouder and happier I became.

 PACK UP YOUR SORROWS IN YOUR
OLD KIT BAG AND SMILE, SMILE, SMILE

Be careful what you wish for.

I thought that if I birthed intelligent babies, they would automatically grow up to be kind and honest and emotionally mature contributing members of society. But then what could one expect of a child having children?

The intelligence I got. More than I bargained for. My third child, Jay, was born January 6, 1962, five years after his sister. Had I been content with two babies, the marriage might have ended sooner. How different my path might have been.

At ten months my infant decided he wanted to walk, so he did with very little groping from table to chair to human leg. At twelve months it was past time for him to talk. So he did. In phrases, not single words. Eventually nonstop. I described him as a walking encyclopedia. His attitude toward sports, musical instruments was the same: he could do anything he wanted, without help. For the most part he was right,

Except for swimming. One summer afternoon, at Buttermilk Falls State Park, he watched his older brother, Fred, jump into the pool, and he did likewise. Fortunately the lifeguard was watching and rescued him.

When he was five, a visiting friend of mine remarked how nervous Jay was. He had just awakened from his nap when she arrived, but an hour later, he was still cranky, whining, interrupting us constantly, unwilling to accept any of my suggestions or attention. She suggested counseling; it was three years since his father had dropped out of his life, and his anger and unhappiness, which started during that time, had grown and grown. It would take a small army to get him in the car. Knowing I wanted him to go, he refused. What dawned on me is that I was emotionally disturbed and needed therapy. So I went.

> The value of therapy
> Is so that, one day,
> When you knock on yourself,
> Somebody answers.
> ~JM

\* \* \*

The road began to straighten significantly for me that year. I discovered I needed counseling as much as my son did; maybe more. And so I slowly, painstakingly put away my fictional life and replaced it with one of value. I went to the Mental Health Clinic in Ithaca, and they connected me to two wonderful therapists: Charlotte Fogel and then Jeanne O'Rear. They charged on a sliding scale, so the therapy cost me very little. For almost seven years, therapy taught me about myself.

## THE BEST AND WORST OF TIMES

> superimposed on starched lace
> drying on adjustable curtain stretchers
> I see impaled women
> in jogging shoes
> still washed out
> full of holes
> singing like thorn birds
> while trying to clean
> the blood of motherhood
> wife doctor lawyer
> and chief
> off thin exhausted bodies.
> ~JM

\* \* \*

As my health improved, I looked around for ways to increase my income. Society found me superfluous. Problems with my spine left me unable to perform physical labor for more than a short while at a time.

The Civil Rights movement of the late sixties and early seventies provided for me what my family, my marriage, my religion, my educational system denied me: a chance to grow, to learn, to heal myself – by helping others. My volunteer activities in Jack Goldman's organization, MOVE, helping black and low-income families, people who faced discrimination, find decent housing in the area, not only allowed me the opportunity to find myself but the work turned into a paying job.

Becoming an active member of MOVE presented me challenging opportunities to express my deep love for other cultures, and to use the innate, inherent intelligence that was rarely recognized in me. By interacting with other like-minded people of all backgrounds and talents, I learned that nothing is impossible. That if I didn't have an answer to a challenge, to a problem, just pretend, and the knowledge, help, opportunity surfaced.

What can be more thrilling than to help a family become a homeowner? Especially a family of three or four generations living in a crowded, poorly maintained apartment, or having to move often for various reasons. Or an employed but low-income mother that banks overlooked for racial or financial or gender reasons. Alan Treman, president of the Tompkins County Trust Company, listened to me, found my reasoning plausible, and worked out mortgages for three women I brought in.

Another service I offered to people looking for apartments, furniture, clothing, or moral support was MOVE's Housing Information Service. People called me at home, telling me what size apartment they wanted, what neighborhood. I gave them the information other volunteers had gathered.

What was surprising was that some MOVE members convinced United Way to pay me a small salary for this service!

By 1972, the Human Rights Commission was active; discrimination was illegal. In 1977, Ithaca Neighborhood Housing Services began to reverse the deterioration of homes in the city of Ithaca by fixing them up, rather than tearing them down, and providing low-cost loans for new homeowners. MOVE had accomplished its original goal: to move out old thinking and behavior patterns.

\* \* \*

After a year or so, others saw what I couldn't; I was winding down. Trying to humanize the welfare system, racist landlords and discriminating financial institutions was proving too much for me and so I was replaced.

Now, what would I do? I wondered. How would I support myself and my children? I fantasized about being in print. I agonized over the jobs I knew I could do but for which society demanded the proper credentials.

> When I was young,
> I lived in a world that made statements
> with periods at the end.
> Now I live in a world
> that knows only how to ask questions.
> What will I teach my children?
> ~JM

Then, from one of the families I was involved with before I left my job, I learned that an income property on South Cayuga Street, where I used to play as a child, was on the market.

It was in great shape. When I was helping others buy homes, I had learned to check the plumbing, wiring, foundation, roof-line, in other words, whether the house was up to code or not. The house would allow me a wee bit of income while I could still care for my troubled family.

It would provide home maintenance learning skills for my teenage children. It was the road to financial freedom, thinking that in later years I might buy more property. Borrowing the down payment from Mom and taking money from my savings account for closing costs, I bought the three-apartment house in August, 1971. It proved a good thing – stressful, but good.

\* \* \*

Interesting that U.S. politics reflected personal politics. Patty Hearst was abducted, later joined her abductors to help rob a San Francisco bank. Faced with impeachment, Nixon resigned over the Watergate scandal. On a sad violin note, in 1974, beloved Jack Benny died at 80. I, too, wanted to die. That bottle of tranquilizers suddenly became my best friend. Fortunately there were other best friends in my life. One was a woman who urged me to take the few credits I had earned at Cornell, transfer them to enroll as a part time student at TC-3.

I needed a great deal of encouragement to try again. One course a semester at Cornell was too much. I was crying in public, terrified of failing, though I never did, exhausted all the time.

"TC-3 is different," my friend insisted. "There's little pressure; you're with a more diverse student body; you can take courses at night, once a week, rather than three times a week. Try it."

"But I'm depressed. I have no energy. How can I do the reading? The writing?"

"Try it. Each experience is different. Don't judge today by yesterday."

"Where will I get the energy? I also am disabled; I have a defective vertebra that slips out of place when I act too normal. I'm in too much pain."

"So take one course. One night a week."

Becoming REAL meant I was as important as my children, maybe more so. At least to me. I was a just, gentle parent. If he could not accept my limits; it would be my Jay who left, not me. I could taste the Bachelor of Science degree, wanting one so badly. But, of course, my fear of once again failing turned the taste sour. Until 1972 when that spoonful of encouragement got me to take a summer Biology course at the new Community College 15 miles away.

Surprised as hell, passing Biology 101, 102 I had to drop, too many headaches. Somehow, despite my constant fear of failure, despite the death of my mother, despite getting to the point where that whole bottle of tranquilizers on my bedside table began to look as a good way out of all my dead-end struggles to help my ever more challenged young son; despite having to deal with chauvinistic institutions in finding another place for that son to live, despite flooded creeks, washed out roads, snow storms and crying storms, going part-time for 3 years, I graduated Magna Cum Laude in January 1975 – A.S. in Science. I knew my shadow was taller!

For a short while, my dream of a masters in – what? English? Or Creative Writing? – seemed possible. I enrolled in Empire State College, a school without walls. A learning institution that would give me credit for my life experiences. From my ever-continuing therapy, from my reading, from my work, I felt I knew about child-development, Italian studies, sociology, psychology, home buying, affective education, cooking, women's studies. I wanted the opportunity to put my money where my mouth was, to write up my knowledge and get credit for it. But I was no match for chauvinistic mentors, inflation, severe back pain, and ever increasing lack of energy. I gave in and eventually gave up – save for an occasional course in Psycho-Biography or American Madness at Cornell.

\* \* \*

Reading Betty Friedan's book *The Feminine Mystique* was very frustrating. There was so much to identify with. What prompted me to put my frustration down on paper was what she wrote about the American woman-mother, hopping from one task to another, never able to spend more than 15 minutes on one task, be it dishwashing, doing laundry, or vacuuming. No wonder, when she finally sits down to read, she can spend only 15 minutes; then her attention wanders on to something else, or she falls asleep, exhausted from the many roles she plays each day and every day.

Finding this problem of the 15-minute attention-span to be one of the many I have had to deal with as I made, and continue to make, the transition back to woman-student from mother-nobody, counseling helped. I noticed I could sit and read for a much longer period of time. The fact that I enjoyed my classes and the reading made the adjustment a little easier. Now I can sit and read, even though there's laundry to do, or clothes to fold, or a dishwasher to load, and ignore all of it as I engross myself in my reading or writing.

# SOMEWHERE OVER THE RAINBOW

The bottle of tranquilizers on my night table beside my bed seems to be flashing a green light. Go. Take me. Swallow all of me. I'll feel peaceful, relaxed. Those feelings will last forever. I won't ever have to deal again with the possibility of Jay arguing with me for hours about bedtime, or letting his sister's rabbits out of their cages, or stealing his older brother's allowance, or beating up his younger brother tomorrow morning as he's done for the past six months. Furthermore there will be no more loud discussions over ripped jeans, string beans, or his meat being too close to his potatoes.

The hopelessness and despair fill my bedroom like poisonous gas seeping out from every corner, every floorboard, every drawer. Every article of clothing hanging in my closet waves to me, "Have a safe trip." Outside the moon passes behind clouds, the window becomes black.

The bucket, the pail, the bushel, the cupboard are empty. Like the old woman who lived in a shoe, I have nothing more to feed my son. I am totally empty. So empty that the only solution is to fill myself with more emptiness – just to cease to exist.

I am 39 and am a part-time student at Tompkins Cortland Community College. Doing very well. But I don't fool very many. There are those who can see behind my eyes and feel the exhaustion, hear the sadness. There are others who notice my walk, the carriage of my head, know that my body is getting tighter and tighter every day. They feel my pain as I try bending or stooping. I think the exhausting lower back pain is from my defective fifth lumbar vertebra that an X-ray revealed, but it is really the muscles that are being screwed tighter and tighter by a twelve-year-old screwdriver. Every day. Every day.

\* \* \*

"I'm not a quitter," I say to myself and to whomever just might be listening. Committing suicide is a most unfunny joke to play on someone you claim to love. When he finally grows up and understands or is told what happened, do I really want him to have to deal with all that guilt? And what of the other three? They were abandoned by their father, isn't that enough? If I truly love him, as I say I do, and I feel I have done everything humanly possible to try to help him resolve whatever it is that makes him so angry, then perhaps it is he who should leave home, not me.

I've been instrumental in getting Dean's List recognition for part-time students. My whole life is ahead of me. Next year I graduate. Find Jay, now twelve, a foster home.

\* \* \*

A foster home for Jay could not be found. How nice a private school would be—but I couldn't afford it. His father decided to take him. And I was too sick to argue.

> "You know what," he said to me,
> Brown hair over a changing face
> Brown eyes hiding darkness.
> "Kelly and I seem like strangers, not brothers,
> When we pass at a hockey game.
> I've been wanting to come up to see you.
> Dad says it would be best if I don't.
> Some Saturday I'll drop in."
> I hear the sound of chains mingling
>   With angry smiles, forbidden tears.

Until he was 15, I saw him three or four times at most. One of my futile efforts was when he was hospitalized for peritonitis – and inflammation of the stomach lining. The hospital social worker decided to release him early rather than deal with parental conflicts rumbling at surface's edge.

By 1977, knowing what Jay's life was like and thinking maybe he had learned a bit about self-discipline, I encouraged him to return. He eventually did—long enough for me to, once again, find more suitable living arrangements for him.

Structure – that's what he needs. What do I need? One hundred years' rest. Mothers fall apart too, you know: Like washing machines, stoves, cars.

I felt I was rejecting him again. Telling him he's no good. Go away. I don't want you. Knowing his school counselor, I turned to him and received kindness, respect, objectivity and help. I had to act fast because to place him in a Group Home here in Tompkins County before he turned 16 – a couple of months away. From all I was told, I felt that was an answer to my prayers: he would receive objective structure, limits, guidance, kindness, tutoring, recreation, life skills, and more. As difficult as it was, I was relieved and grateful to have found such a safe, non-abusive place for my son. Perhaps he would make it to adulthood after all.

\* \* \*

A year later, Jay chose to come back into my life. Back into family court, back into World War III, back into mind confusing headaches, back aches, stomach cramps. I had no energy, my mind wouldn't function, my memory didn't work – I couldn't retain a phone number, remember directions or carry on a meaningful conversation. I was waking up in the middle of the night, terrified, but of what? I didn't know. I couldn't stand being alone but I didn't know why. I had actually learned to make some of my dreams come true. I had traveled a bit; to Russia and Morocco. I had given my anger and sadness to the wind and refilled the spaces with self-understanding. I was learning to accept the unacceptable.

I knew that life was too much for me. I had a total of five rental houses at one point. I couldn't handle the stress that owning income property caused. I had to sell to save myself – from what or for what I didn't know. All I knew was that I was more important than the money. If I wasn't around, the money wouldn't do me or my children any good.

I finally realized that my practical side interfered with my creative needs. While I was coming unglued, I was beginning to be aware that I wanted to be published, that my journals were of value, as is. Not as fiction or rewritten into novels but as one of the oldest forms of writing, one of the few avenues women had to express their humanity, to be creative, to hang on to reality, to say "I am".

In the spring of 1979, a conversation with a doctor informed me that I was depressed. My inability to walk even a block without severe body pain, the uncontrollable crying, the memory loss, my panic and terror were all the result of long years of stress. I was put on a mood stabilizer and warned that I probably wouldn't be aware of any improvement for at least six weeks. The fact that I could hope, that I could once again, some time, maybe not for years, but never the less, sometime, feel like the fourth of July again, helped me to begin to improve almost immediately.

 NO EMPTY NEST SYNDROME FOR ME

1. When did I begin to feel old?
   At eight or nine when I first menstruated and felt scared, ashamed, had no one to turn to or ask.

2. When did I reach my prime?
   I haven't reached it yet. My memory is back, my freedom from childcare loosens the step, lets the foot press down on the gas pedal longer, more often. I am young again; free and responsible, loving and loved, comfortable in my home, my daughter's or son's apartment, or my lover's home.

3. Has time run out for me now that I'm 43?
   Gee! I don't think so. I have a whole new career to commence, dreams to turn to realities, miles to walk.

4. Now that the children are gone, what will I do with all the time?
   Revel in the joy. Sit with my feet up and watch the leaves turn. Write, read, organize. Listen to the genius in me, as Goethe says. Boldness has genius, power, and magic in it. I feel magical, powerful. Not a genius, but close. Maybe.

# I'VE GOT TO BE ME

The more I heal, the further back into my life I'm able to look and see signs of memory loss accompanying my dis-ease. The first conscious awareness that something was wrong with my memory came to me in the 1980s, when I was in my forties and no longer knew how to spell words with which I'd been perfectly familiar. In particular, I remember struggling with *proceed*, *recede*, and *succeed*. Their proper spellings were simply lost to me. Having always been a good speller, I was puzzled by this, but never questioned why it was happening.

Neither did I question my forgetting my nametag for Friday night square dancing, or leaving my key in the door whenever I returned home. Or forgetting faces, names, how I knew the people who spoke to me, phone numbers, grocery lists, and directions to places I have driven to for the past thirty-five years. It was at this same time that I began getting lost—in my own hometown, where I'd lived all my life, so far.

And yet I could still square dance. I could take care of my historic home and my financial affairs. Best of all, I managed to heal myself, totally, of depression, with psychotherapy, when professionals believed there was no known cure.

I guess I thought that whatever was happening, it would self-correct. I never get colds; I've had only one flu shot in my life, and I have no problem with arthritis, diabetes, high blood pressure, or cholesterol.

But looking back farther still in my life, I now recognize much earlier life events and symptoms of the onset of disease. I believe there was cell deterioration going on, even at that young an age, and yet I never stopped and told myself, "Something's wrong here."

In the springtime of 2006, I began to experience brain functions that I have not been able to accomplish since my teenage years—that is, to disagree with something a sibling, a friend, or a professional says to me. The words were never able to make it out of the gate, so to speak. The more I became aware of it, the more frustrated I became. Sometimes it didn't matter; it was no big deal. But now, in my healing years, when I disagree philosophically with someone's' beliefs or behavior, I am able to express myself in a polite, non-critical manner.

The words are now surfacing.

# SELF-ASSESSMENT

*SYMPTOMS*

- ⋆ Poor judgment
- ⋆ Lost the ability to spell familiar words
- ⋆ Lost the ability to retain information
- ⋆ Lost the ability to recall memories or information
- ⋆ Lack of energy
- ⋆ Great nervousness
- ⋆ Lost memory of the names of people I knew well
- ⋆ Lost the ability to remember numbers and faces
- ⋆ Lost memories of why and from where I knew people
- ⋆ Lost the ability to do simple math problems in my head
- ⋆ Lost awareness of obvious connections
- ⋆ Devastating depression
- ⋆ Getting lost while driving
- ⋆ Chronic pain

*MIND-BODY CONNECTIONS:*
*Physical problems affect our mind and spirits.*

- ⋆ The blow to my coccyx, which is connected to the spine and central nervous system, created neurological damage
- ⋆ The stress and abuse in my home, both growing up and in my marriage, negatively affected my overall health

THERAPIES: *Healing one's mind helps heal body and spirit.*
- Chiropractic with Dr. Pierre Gremaud and with Dr. Bernie Graham
- Dowsing to discern beneficial supplements
- Nutritional support and improved diet
- Yoga
- Singing, Dancing, Storytelling and Silence – The Way of the Shaman
- Reading and applying what I learned to my life
- Use of flower essences
- Psychotherapy
- Cranial sacral therapy
- Journal writing
- Replacing negative thoughts with positive thoughts
- Letting go of worry
- Exercise
- Past life regression
- Trager therapy

SIGNS OF HEALING
- Many days in a row of feeling calm and at peace
- Recalling names
- Remembering my relationship to people I meet in public
- Ability to remember phone numbers
- Ability to do simple math problems in my head
- Improved spelling
- Appropriate reactions to situations
- Healed from depression
- Freed from years of anger and resentments
- Information surfacing automatically
- Becoming more politically active
- Complete healing of damaged fifth lumbar vertebra
- Making better decisions
- Doing more gardening
- Experiencing greater joy
- Eternal gratitude

 LET THE SUNSHINE IN

In the 1970s, I met Mabel Beggs, one of the founders of the Foundation of Light in Ithaca. With Kate and John Payne she started a meditation and healing group in the Payne's house. In 1974 they moved their activities to the schoolhouse donated by Mabel Beggs, and incorporated as The Foundation of Light.

It is a free church, a spiritual center for meditation, healing and study. Their purpose is to promote spiritual understanding and practice as found in all great religions in accordance with Cosmic Law. This includes the study and practice of meditation, the study of less understood regions of human potential, research into spiritual healing, investigation into the influence of natural foods on physical well-being and spiritual development, and the development of individual creativity in art, music and literature.

For the past forty years this organization has played a vital role in my healing journey.

\* \* \*

When I need help it shows up—in fascinating ways. One of my chosen contributions to the Foundation of Light was to help order books for members and for the magnificent library established by Kate Payne. These books introduced me to previously unknown worlds of ideas, knowledge, and possibilities. A flier for a book by Dr. Dharma Singh Khalsa, *Brain Longevity*, was included in an order, and when I read it, I knew I had to own the book.

Instead of the printed word, however, I received the book on tape. Months later, I understood what a blessing that "mistake" was. With a dysfunctional memory, trying to read and remember instructions created so much anxiety for me, it made an impossible situation even worse. But *listening* to the words removed the stress, and I recognized the "mistake" of the book on tape as a particular gift.

Dr. Khalsa explains that stressful experiences, as well as the way we deal with them, cause excess cortisol to flood the brain. When that happens constantly, the adrenal glands, which produce cortisol, get disrupted and keep producing it—even when we don't feel stressed.

The excess cortisol interferes with the brain's neurotransmitters—the chemicals that help make connections in our brains. So it's harder to think, and to remember things. The cortisol also allows too much calcium to enter the brain, which produces free radicals, which can kill brain cells.

Dr. Khalsa calls this Age Associated Memory Impairment. He tells us that excess cortisol—plus age-related reduction in important hormones, neurotransmitters, proteins, hydrochloric acid, enzymes, and minerals—contribute to cell damage and memory loss.

Now that I better understand my own life , and as I hear more about memory impairment in children, college students, baby boomers and elders alike, I can no longer accept the idea that memory loss is strictly an age-related problem. Have you wondered at the increasing cases of Alzheimer's in today's world? Stress is a major culprit behind this disease, and stress is a chronic problem in our society. There's a pattern of serious health issues emerging from our increasingly (and deteriorating) "processed" culture, including stress-related disorders: things like insomnia, weight gain, headaches, and cardiovascular problems. Dr. Khalsa's insights are extremely seminal, and he provides valuable solutions that include suggested supplements, dietary modifications, and physical, mental, and breathing exercises.

# TURN TURN TURN

Reviewing all the supplements Dr. Khalsa suggested confused me. But at the Foundation of Light, I learned a method that helps me decide, each day, what supplements I need. I dowse for guidance.

I know there are those who would shake their heads at the very concept of dowsing. It doesn't seem scientific, in an age when science is the supreme god. But human consciousness is an ever-changing phenomenon, and there have always been its two threads. The best way I can think of to describe them is: the spiritual, that is, everything non-scientific; and the material, that is, everything within the realm of science.

At different times in human history, one thread or the other has been dominant. It would be incorrect, however, to suggest that one thread negates the existence of the other, and there are great thinkers today who believe that human consciousness is once again in transition, this time evolving to a state in which equal weight is to be given to both those threads.

Dowsing isn't quite the mystery some would make it out to be. It simply connects with the unconscious mind, as do the I Ching or Tarot cards. I'm not talking about using sticks or rods to dowse for water or oil, although people successfully do that. Instead, I use a pendulum—a small crystal or bead on a thread or chain.

Here's how it works. First, you cleanse the crystal by washing it in salt water. Then you sit quietly and center yourself, breathing quietly and deeply, relaxing your muscles. If you have a higher power to call on, that will help too.

Hold the thread so it's 4 to 6 inches long and the bead or crystal can swing freely. Now discover how your "yes" or "no" answers happen. You can say something that is incorrect, like "My name is Nancy," or you can say "Show me a clear sign for No." The crystal may swing from side to side, forward and backward, on a slant, or even in a circle. Everyone is different. Then you do the same thing to discover the "yes" answer: "My name is Jemma," or "Show me a clear sign for Yes." Every morning, I hold my dowsing crystal over each bottle of supplements, flower essences, and essential oils (more about those later), and ask of each, "Will I benefit from this today?"

I continue without fail to take what is beneficial. How you word your question is very important, as it must be worded without ambiguity in order to elicit a yes or no answer. I recommend *Dowsing for Health*, by Patrick Macmanaway, M.D., as a good source for learning more about this fascinating subject. I wouldn't be here without Mabel Beggs and Kate Payne of the Foundation of Light, who taught me how to dowse.

As you read about the various healing methods I explain below, you might be saying that you can't afford alternative healing. Even though insurance in the United States doesn't always cover these kind of therapies, I'm sure that over the years I—or my insurance company— have spent less money on my health than I would have with allopathic medicine. In my quest to heal myself, I could have spent hundreds of thousands of dollars on tests, surgeries, and a medicine cabinet full of drugs. I'd have five or six specialist physicians, none of them talking with one another. And my quality of life would be much worse.

 I NEVER PROMISED YOU A ROSE GARDEN

What amazes me about my relationship with my friend Dorothy Lonsky is that the two times she suggested a complementary therapy, I immediately made an appointment, without even knowing anything about whatever it was she was suggesting. Though we disagree about other things in life, in this area, when she speaks, I jump.

The first time was in 1986, when she told me about Trager therapy, which concerns itself with finding restrictions in the membrane along the cranial sutures and restoring a free flow of the cerebrospinal fluid from the cranium to the coccyx and out through the nerves to the rest of the body. This therapy allows the body to restore its balance and heal.

Milton Trager M.D. (1908-1997) was himself born with a congenital spinal deformity. He worked to overcome his difficulty despite weakness and a great deal of sickness throughout his childhood. In his late teens, he began training as a boxer. It was at that time that he had his first experience of intuitively accessing a body workout technique that produced the results that would come to be known as the Trager Approach.

Trager's trainer always rubbed him down following each boxing session. But one day, noticing that his trainer looked particularly tired, Milton offered him the rubdown instead. The man was astonished by what he experienced at the young man's hands. Milton, encouraged by the positive results achieved on his trainer, went home and offered the rubdown to his father, who experienced the same sense of well-being.

Thus began the exploration that lasted his entire life. Milton offered his approach to anyone open to experiencing it. People suffering from as wide a range of difficulties as emphysema, asthma, multiple sclerosis, muscular dystrophy, polio and painful backs—all responded, in degrees ranging from greater physical ease to the miraculous. In his early exploration, Milton applied this approach to a nineteen-year-old friend who had polio and was confined to a wheelchair. That friend was soon walking again, after four years of paralysis.

There are two aspects of the Trager Approach. In one, referred to as the tablework, the client is passive. In the other, called Mentastics, the client is active. Using gentle, non-intrusive and natural movements, the tablework helps the body release deep physical and mental patterns. These patterns might be in response to an accident, illnesses, or any kind of emotional or physical trauma—even "just" the stress of everyday life. Releasing these patterns facilitates deep relaxation, increased physical mobility, and mental clarity. This experience of effortless movement is maintained and reinforced by Mentastics, simple, active, self-induced movements possible in the course of daily activities.

*Moving Medicine*, by Jack Liskin, is an excellent biography of Dr. Trager and his life. The book is available from the Trager Institute. Here's an article I wrote for The Trager Newsletter.

# THE CAPACITY FOR BETTER THINGS

*Basta! 50 years was long enough to be ill. I had been silent long enough; I wanted to be well, not a woman of the shadows like all the other Italians I know. I wanted to be an Italian-American woman whose name was in lights and on everyone's lips. I wanted to make up for all the years, the lifetime my mother spent locked up in la miseria because she was woman born. And the same for my sad, enduring father who made certain his children were born here in the land with the golden doors. And his sister who spent 38 years in a mental hospital – depressed and mute. But she could crochet anything.*

*I wanted to crochet words into people's hearts and memories. When a local writer won a Pulitzer, I asked, why couldn't it be me? In order to do that, my mind and body had to function more than one hour a day. Ideas had to be able to make the leap from nerve-ending to nerve-ending. I had to be able to hold a pen, to break with the Italian tradition of not exposing oneself, not advancing oneself, not bringing attention to oneself. I needed life flowing through my body to think of fresh ways to say things, to stop being only a diarist and to become, also, a poet, an author.*

*Oh how I had tried! I divorced, went into therapy, un-became female. I left the church, furthered my education. I gave up custody of a child, improved my diet. I accepted a mood stabilizer and slept half the 80's away.*

*Much of that was all incredibly helpful and worthwhile but, still, I was horizontal most of the time, unable to work, or be with my grandbabies or commit myself to a project. Changing my bed weekly was a major event that often stretched to 9 or 10 days because I was too tired or I couldn't remember when I last changed it. And I wouldn't think of trying to go out for groceries the same day. If I wanted to go square dancing, I rested for days to have the energy. Was I ever going to get over the learned despair?*

*Jacob Riis, a 19ᵗʰ century photographer said: "There is that about the Italian woman that suggests the capacity for better things." I had been living that belief a long time, knowing there are no absolutes, knowing if I just keep trying, a way would find me.*

*Must be it was that 'capacity for better things' that dialed the number, made the appointment for my first Trager session. All I knew is that my limbs would be manipulated, gently moved, and that it was "something." Didn't make sense but I was willing.*

*That was in late August, 1986. Two weeks and two sessions later, on September 4ᵗʰ, I had the notion to go to bed without the lavender circle of magic that kept me from crying uncontrollably, feeling sorry for myself, and worse.*

*I tried giving up the pills a month ago, I told myself, and six months ago and a year. So try it again. Put the pill bottle and water on your nightstand – just in case.*

*The next morning, when I awoke, I felt as though I had caught the wind and changed its direction. I still do.*

*That hooked me. I didn't know how Trager psycho-physical integration therapy works; only that it had. I knew I had to go weekly to get the reinforcement, the re-education, the whatever it was I was receiving so that one day I would speak Health. It became very clear to me months before I ever heard of Milton Trager, that even though I understood what was wrong with me, I was stuck. I couldn't help myself anymore than what I had already accomplished. I didn't have the energy.*

*That first day, while my body was being shaken (as a friend recently put it) I "felt" myself being rocked in a cradle. Was Trager therapy picking up where my lonely mother left off? Was I reclaiming my infancy and childhood, this time in health? I didn't have time to think about it because I next found myself in a "Primitive Society" listening to the drums and watching the dancing. Bare feet on bare Mother Earth. Is that the way early people kept themselves free of tension and stress? Did I do that in a former life? Was Trager therapy a modern adaptation?*

*Feminine Earth energy is protective and healing. Eventually my body felt it and responded in wondrous fashion. My arms discovered they could move around to express an idea I was talking about and not feel awkward or self-conscious or silly. My torso discovered music of its own making and I started dancing inside my skin.*

*Jokingly often referring to myself as good for nothing, how could the price improve? It did. My appetite has all but vanished, making it next to impossible to take me out to dinner. Concerned that one day I might look under the sheet to find I had either disappeared or turned into a toothpick, my therapist calmed me by saying my body was seeking its own level.*

*Remembering Italian genes are good for something, I relaxed and enjoyed all the stares — now that my days have lengthened and I am out more and more in the noon day sun, not to mention the evening.*

*The cat no longer has my tongue. I speak out — politely — and I love it. Inch-by-inch I am becoming gayer than laughter.*

*Back under the sheet while my body cells continue to forget past, unpleasant, and painful experiences, and the resultant tension, I feel safe, secure, knowing no great harm will come to me. That's good to know, especially when I see a "you've got to be crazy look" in some questioning people's expressions when I tell them about my weight loss or why my eyes sparkle, my skin glows, and there seems to be this profound sense of inner peace in me.*

*Well, that helps, I smile back at those looking at me oddly. It helps with writing poetry, why not with living poetry?*

## INTERIOR DECORATING

Leapfrogging
over present models
of myself,
I fast-forward
Star Trek-like
traveling light years
in reverse
with every Trager session.

Shedding layer upon layer
of unmemorable experiences
that hold me a prisoner
with gossamer chains,
I am a pioneer on my own
forging over old wagon trails
that self-destruct
as I zoom by.
~JM

 YOU'LL NEVER WALK ALONE

With the injury to my sacrum still affecting my whole system, I found that CranioSacral Therapy (CST) helped me to continue releasing both physical and emotional pain. I went to see Nancy Young at her Healing Tree Studio. She would put her hands on my skull and gently free the cranial sutures and the spinal fluids, which flow from the base of the spine to the tailbone or sacrum. She works with the "dural pulse," the rhythm and energy of our cerebro-spinal fluid.

In fact, Nancy, who is also a medical intuitive, told me that I was younger than 13 when my mother kicked me. She not only helped to realign my body, she also helped me release the tension and emotional pain from my injury.

Nancy explained that CST was developed by Dr. John E. Upledger. From 1975 to 1983, he was a professor of biomechanics at the College of Osteopathic Medicine at Michigan State University. With a team of other scientists, including anatomists, physiologists, biophysicists and bioengineers, he did clinical research that led to CranioSacral Therapy. After her training at the Upledger Clinic in Florida, Nancy worked there as an assistant therapist.

Here is what Nancy writes about CST:

> By complementing the body's natural healing processes, CST is increasingly used as a preventive health measure for its ability to bolster resistance to disease, and is effective for a wide range of medical problems associated with pain and dysfunction.

With Nancy's medical intuition complementing her training and experience, she helped me to continue my task of releasing years of emotional and physical pain.

\* \* \*

As I was working with Dr. Khalsa's tape and participating with the breathing and Kundalini yoga, another world of healing opened for me that I hadn't even known I needed. The more yoga I did, the worse the pain. It felt as if someone had gone in and broken the bones, leaving the skin intact. Getting out of bed each morning or even just turning over or twisting my body was painful. Yet the more yoga I did, the more pain I experienced in my lower back—so much so that I had to stop the yoga and seek help.

Enter my friend Dorothy Lonsky, who dropped in for a visit in April of 1998, after receiving a spinal network adjustment from Dr. Pierre Gremaud. I sought him out. While examining me, he said "there's a trauma there that is at least 30, 35 years old." Amazed at what a light touch to my coccyx could reveal, I told him, "that trauma is about 50 years old, the result of a kick." What amazed me even more was to relive the experience when I was face down on the table, with no expectations or understanding of how touches, often feather light, could release long-held trauma from my body tissue. From memory.

It took only a few weeks, of three adjustments per week, to fully release that trauma which I had long ago psychologically processed, and forgiven my mother. But new pains took the place of old pains. They came and they went. And then they stayed. In the same place, across my lower back.

\* \* \*

Blessed be! Another brilliant chiropractor named Jesse Jutkowitz did extensive research and put together what he calls Advanced Bio-Structural Corrections (ABC). Pierre trained with him, and I started the new protocol in the fall of 2002. ABC addresses pathologies in the spinal column, which can twist and bend. These pathologies occur in three dimensions—not two, as other treatments assume—and ABC provides three-dimensional treatment of the spinal column. It results in consistent and predictable corrections of spinal curvatures.

With ABC I experience days of absolute calmness—something totally new to me. I also experience improved memory and days of unending energy.

And more pain in my coccyx, so much so that I could not sit very long in any one position. It reminded me of the exact pain I experienced as a teenager when I was kicked. At first I thought I would eventually process it out as I received ABC corrections, but the pain persisted.

When I complained to Pierre he suggested I have Somatic Respiratory Integration (SRI) sessions with Rene Beck. SRI is a healing method that helps the brain reconnect with the body by using a simple touch, breathing, and movement technique. Its exercises are intended to reconnect rhythmic breathing with awareness of the body. The goal is to shift one's consciousness to support trust for the mind-body connection and the healing process. SRI also promotes increased peace and ease.

Under constant stress, the body actually takes on defensive postures that result in spinal distortion, among other things. SRI exercises consistently relieve the defensive posture of spinal distortion and the disconnection of body/mind relationship. Its benefits include:

- Unlocking the body's natural healing ability
- Reconnecting mind, body, and spirit
- Reducing stress
- Freeing up significant amounts of energy
- Releasing emotion stored in the body on a cellular level

What I discovered during the breathing exercise is that I had not dealt with the anger, sadness, inappropriate behavior and other feelings still stored inside me after all those years. It was my dear, lonely, unhappy mother, full of anger herself, who had caused my suffering. While I lay on the floor breathing, she appeared to my mind's eye. I saw her in profile, wearing her typical 1950s housedress and black-laced shoes, and her black hair in braids. I tell her how I feel, how much I hurt, how much I suffered in silence. She apologizes.

Other unresolved issues surfaced, much to my amazement, and I am dealing with them in appropriate ways.

To my joy, the pain subsided and I now have a way to manage it when it recurs.

# P.S. I LOVE YOU
## 2003

### September 2003

I've done little writing since the beginning of the year. Dreams and meditations inform me to spend the winter, spring, and summer healing. My 60-year dark night of the soul and my children's 40 years of darkness are over . The sounds of healing can be heard throughout the land.

Just in the last five weeks, while dancing – I now jitterbug – I am overjoyed as I observe my body moving in ways it never could before. And when in bed, my legs naturally, totally on their own, stretch out full-length instead of curling up, tensing up, in the fetal position, as they've done for years and years.

My eyesight has improved even more, as has my energy level and my balance. I still have miles to walk before I am home, and perhaps a different therapy, another supplement, a new whatever. It doesn't matter. The enthusiasm, joy, and energy with which I greet each day are proof to me that I am no longer robbing my bank.

### It's a Long Way to Tipperary

How interesting that that song title comes to mind in the middle of the night. Not only have I never been to Tipperary, I haven't heard the song on the radio in decades. And I'm not Irish, my children are. But that's okay. It's a good song to introduce this postscript to *The Bank Robber*.

*The secret to success is to go from failure to failure without losing your enthusiasm.*
*– Winston Churchill*

Tipperary symbolizes home, and if one walks away from home for thirty years or more, it is a long way back. In September, along with resting and not writing, I took a break from the chiropractic treatment with Dr. Gremaud. My neck hurt, my lower back hurt, and my short-term memory was actually worse. I was leaving my keys in the kitchen door again. No sooner would I put a bowl on the table, or decide to write a letter, than a simple interruption—a phone call, for instance—and I'd totally forget what I was doing.

Worse, I was experiencing paranoia—which to me is a deeper, out-of-control level of worry. I had given up worry for Lent, and for every other good reason. But at that time, my brain would not stop repeating over and over conversations I'd had with someone, or a silly idea, like "They don't like me." I had become a broken record.

On one of my neighborhood streets there is a yellow brick line that lies under the cement and blacktop. It is rumored to have influenced L. Frank Baum, the author of *The Wizard of Oz*, who visited Ithaca while he was writing the beloved tale. This time it was the Good Witch who came to my rescue. Her husband, Dr. Bernie Graham, a chiropractor, uses laser therapy, color therapy, nutritional supplements and other adjustments for pain relief and healing.

It is now almost Christmas. For the past month I have been walking the mile to Bernie's office two or three times a week. I notice that I retain names longer. The pain has diminished. My sense of direction is improving, and I have more energy. I visualize digging holes in the earth, burying the pain.

I also visualize more trips to Europe, perhaps a stop in Tipperary.

### Wednesday, New Year's Eve, 2003

For Christ's sake, why can't I remember her name? We are both at the Burning Bowl ceremony held annually at the Foundation of Light, one of the organization's most popular rituals. Participants burn scraps of paper on which they have written behavior patterns they do not wish to take into the new year. Then they write letters to themselves stating what they expect to experience, accomplish, etc.

For some reason I can never remember her name, even thought I hear it monthly at other events we both attend. Darn! I cannot even remember the plan I had devised to help me recall her name. It is not a difficult name, of that I am certain. It is a name with which I am familiar. Does it rhyme with Mary? Or Sue? Or Chris?

Oh, I know! It is the same as a childhood classmate's. Whose? Presently the light switch in my head turns on, but there is a delay in the power surge. Then the name, Hilda, lights up in my brain and my face.

One day, near the end of January, I am absolutely amazed and thrilled to find myself doing a math problem in my head, something I have not been able to do for years.

A few days later, while in conversation with a relative, a question relevant to a past discussion surfaces unexpectedly in my mind. I am overjoyed. I also find myself remembering phone calls and faces.

### Saturday, January 2004

Years ago, she lived in an apartment across the street from me. We spoke often, and at one point she considered renting from me. Since she moved I see her once a year at the Twelfth Night celebration at the Unitarian Church. I always remember her name.

So why is tonight different, especially since my memory is improving? I recognize her face. Why is her name playing hide-and-seek? I am not tired or in great pain that saps my energy. I love listening to the made-up stories the attendees share, and to friends and acquaintances – old and new – catching up on one another's lives.

Deciding not to dwell on it, I relax. Presently I can feel the wheel turning in my brain. Cells ask other cells: where did we store that name? It has to be here someplace. We used it last year. Oh yes! Here it is. Hatice. My eyes light up – of course.

# BUDDY, CAN YOU SPARE A DIME?

Do you believe in karma? The idea that what goes around comes around? The philosophy that everything we do, for lifetime after lifetime, is recorded, and that there is no kindness forgotten or transgression not paid for?

Karma is part of the Eastern philosophy that each soul goes through countless incarnations on its evolutionary path toward perfection. In each lifetime, we experience exactly what we need. And we return in groups so that those who received from us in one lifetime can return the favors—good or bad—in the next lifetime. Or over many lifetimes, it seems, in my case.

I believe in this. Sort of. How else to explain my lifelong attraction to men with drinking problems when, not only do I not drink, there's no evidence of any drinking problems in my family. My father didn't drink. There was never wine on our table. I have no use for it. I am not an enabler or a rescuer. But whether the man in my life was a gifted surgeon, a therapist, or a nurse, there was always this *ménage a trois*.

Growing up (or not growing up) in the '40s and '50s, "nice girls" didn't touch the stuff. I preferred root beer and sodas. So why did I end up with a husband who was an alcoholic? We divorced before his dependency became debilitating, but he died at age 50 of cirrhosis of the liver and cancer. One could chalk that learning experience to my youth, my lack of understanding about such things, a lack of parental guidance.

Or karma?

As demonstrated throughout this book, I spent long years examining my life, where I was, where I wanted to be, and how I was going to get there. One mammoth issue was my religion, which didn't accept divorce and remarriage. It took me a number of years, but help came in the form of books by theologians such as SØren Kierkegaard and Teilhard de Chardin, to name two that I remember.

Catholicism slowly lost its grip on me as I read about natural law, books excluded from the Bible, about Roman and Greek myths and their similarities to our religious myths. I also studied concepts such as love and compassion and forgiveness, and where heaven exists, if at all.

All that learning was a walk in the park compared to my non-love affairs with alcohol and men dependent on it. All through the '60s, '70s, '80s, and right up to the mid-'90s, most of the men in my life had drinking problems. Some friends said it was normal, to accept the fact that men drink, that "boys will be boys."

I didn't.

Others didn't notice it.

I did.

When asked why I don't drink, my response is: when the children were little, I couldn't afford it. Now that they are grown, I don't need it.

John Bradshaw, in his book *Coming Home*, does a wonderful job explaining his battle with the stuff, how he dealt with it, and how he helps others. Reading his book, I thought surely I could meet someone who could take a drink of wine at dinner—or not—and be content.

Having learned to stop blaming others for my problems or life challenges, and seeing them as opportunities for growth, achievement, transcendence, why the enduring non-love affair with the bottle? What was I doing wrong? Or, to be more positive, not right?

By the late '80s, I was asking myself that question, and others. By the '90s, I was reading that we create our own future, that we manifest what we think about. In the last decade before the millennium, I was learning how powerful we humans really are. The problem is, we don't know how to manifest our desires.

One thing I never did was to seek out hypnotherapy, regressive therapy, or a gifted individual who might be able to explain to me why I attracted a certain kind of man. What I did start doing was focusing my thoughts on the positive, not the negative, on creating my own future by "acting as if." I acted as though the problem was already solved. I also paid closer attention to who came into my life. If there was a love of liquor, it ended the friendship immediately. Over time, what changed was the degree of attachment to alcohol my new male friends had. It grew less and less in the men I knew as my determination grew stronger and stronger.

\* \* \*

I recently read *Sacred Contracts* by Caroline Myss, Ph.D., and now I more fully understand why, after I gained my freedom from marriage, I continued to attract into my life men who had affairs with alcohol.

Myss helped me understand that the problem was my Shadow Archetypal pattern repeating itself over and over in my life. I was afraid to love anyone, afraid of the pain of possible loss and grief, so I kept attracting men whom I considered unacceptable.

But at the same time, my thinking, logical brain came up with a plan. Each time I noticed a dependency on booze, I ended the relationship. It took years and years, and what I noticed as those years went by was that the men's dependency grew less and less – until, finally, I had male friends who had no dependency on it at all.

# I GET AROUND

This piece of my journey came to me several years ago. In 1999 my friend David called me one winter day, saying he was gathering together a group for a weekend of healing. David is an integrative therapist himself. Very eclectic. So much so, I haven't a title for what he does. With a dentist for a father, he experienced severe brain poisoning from fluoride treatments in his childhood, and he was still healing. Would I like to join him and the others for the weekend? Of course. I, too, am courageous, or like to think that I am.

Having just recently embarked on my plan of however-long-it-takes to become a Pulitzer Prize writer, my focus for the weekend was to release any beliefs, trauma, negativity, memories, or limits that were interfering with my goal. Though I could not yet see or hear the melodic words dance out of my right hand onto paper, I could taste them. Everyone who gathered together, that winter Saturday morning, heard how single-minded and devoted I was to clearing all obstacles to my new profession.

The facilitator instructed us to lie down on the blankets each of us had brought. We were going to be led in what was basically a breathing exercise—similar to Re-Birthing, I was told. Never having participated in a Re-Birthing session, I had very little to go on other than my eagerness and curiosity, and experience in other healing therapies.

I cleared my mind, breathed deeply, relaxed, and did whatever else I was instructed to do. Soon the tears started dampening my cheeks, running down my face.

Lying very still, breathing in and out, in and out, I began to "see" the flag-draped coffin, the crowds of people, the train that carried my beloved's body back to Springfield, Illinois, from Washington, D.C. Remaining very still, hearing others in the room breathing, I focused on the historic scene playing in my head. Totally surprised by what I was seeing, it nevertheless made sense because twenty years earlier, more or less, I'd been told that I had been a guard at the White House during the Civil War. That I saw President Lincoln every working day. It was during that lifetime that my abiding love for the man was established. Having found that piece of my truth, the depths and clarity of my relationship with Mr. Lincoln has strengthened over time.

Long before I knew about this past life experience, however, there was yet another connection to Lincoln. In 1962, January 6th to be exact, I gave birth to a son, my second. I had the name all picked out: he was to be A. Lincoln Wilcox. Such a distinguished set of consonants and vowels. I loved writing that name. My husband didn't. I didn't launch a counter-attack.

Back on the blanket, on the floor, I visualized letting go of all the pain, sorrow and anger I had been storing in my body tissue all these lifetimes. Next I "saw" John Wilkes Booth's body in black clothing, as he had been found that dark day. Knowing the value of forgiveness—as much and more for the one doing the forgiving as for the person on whom it is bestowed—I cradled the man who was responsible for the greatest loss this country had known, stroking his body with the same hand that had saluted President Lincoln, and spoke to him of sorrow and guilt and self-hate. I told him it was past time for him to forgive himself—especially if he wished to reincarnate.

It is almost impossible to describe such an awesome experience. I believed some significant shift had occurred in my subconscious, and that my writing hand would tell me if that were true.

It was probably my left hand that opened the wide, heavy White House door, and my right hand that saluted Lincoln as he passed in front of me. "Good Morning, Mr. President," I always said, so happy to see him, and yet so sad to see in his face what the war was doing to him. No matter how he felt, he responded with "Good morning, John," and made my day. To be so privileged! I couldn't imagine a better job than mine, except one in which I could be with him more often. Perhaps as his driver, or secretary. If asked, I would have gladly and eagerly stood guard on my days off, on Sundays and holidays and vacation days.

Years and lifetimes later, I wonder if it was my right hand's memory of those years at the White House that prevented my using it to strike my children or anyone at all, ever. How could I ever inflict on another person pain like the pain I felt when I heard of the assassination? My grief could not have been greater had I lost parents and siblings and children in a house fire or a malaria epidemic.

Mr. Lincoln was the tallest man in the whole universe to me. He was the funniest, the most honest and courageous and compassionate, the wisest man on the face of the earth. The memory of my loss, the pain of never again hearing his voice or seeing his sunken, pain-filled eyes, watching his back disappear down the White House hall, or being greeted by his son Will, has lingered in my collective memory. In my bones, tissue, cells. In my soul, which has inhabited a body over and over all these lifetimes.

What an amazing experience I told every one, afterwards. How can that happen? The session was on a Saturday afternoon. Sunday morning I awoke with no pain. Alleluia! The experience has been totally processed. I'm free at last!

Monday morning the pain was back but instead of being confined to the hip areas, it moved around – sometimes in the hips, sometimes in the back. And I felt it off and on all day. It was time to get some professional help from my friend. He had been offering it to me for months but I kept saying, or asking, "Why can't I resolve it myself?"

\* \* \*

Christmas intervened and so my appointment was on Friday, January 14th, 2000. I continued with the regression therapy. The use of a coach or therapist helps you make headway, personally or professionally.

On a table, this time, rather than the floor, as soon as I stretched out, relaxed, cleared my mind, I was right back at the White House and at Lincoln's funeral. More sadness, loss, grief to process. Understanding how important forgiveness and compassion are for personal growth and transformation, when I saw myself holding John Wilkes Booth's black clad body, more tears flowed. How unhappy, disturbed he must have been to do such a violent act. I continued to cradle Wilkes's body, feeling the sadness flow out of me – freeing me.

Though my face looked the part of someone who just lost her best friend, my walk home, seven blocks' worth, was joyful. Spring was blooming inside me. New shoots were pushing up through healthy, lustrous soil. First there's happiness, then joy, then bliss. I was certain I was somewhere between the second and third levels.

While sweeping the sidewalks, again, before my next appointment, I was reminded, that in dreams, snow represents frozen emotions. An usually cold spell made it feel like we were trapped in a freezer. And if the truth were told, a freezer might have been a bit warmer. The back pain had diminished but not all together. Hopefully the next session would do it. Fully expecting to release Lincoln sadness, when my therapist asked me what I was thinking about, I waited to let the images surface: family and siblings.

Eyes closed, breathing deeply and regularly, my mind becomes a birth canal – dark, black, shiny, slippery. Uneventful.

The next scenes I've recalled many times, never as vivid as this. With the wicker picnic basket (which I still have) full of pizza or chicken and lemonade, all made from scratch, Mom often took us by city bus to Stewart Park for an afternoon of swimming in Cayuga Lake, swinging, teeter-tottering, and sliding. Oh yes, she also packed extra clothing in that picnic basket, just in case there was a mud puddle at the end of the slide. My younger brother and I played on everything. Up and down. Up and down.

In the early 40s, before World War II, the States were still experiencing economic depression and unemployed men still rode the rails. They were called Hobos and I'm positive one of them was sitting on a green park bench one sunny afternoon. In work shoes, the cuffs of his clean, cotton pants rolled up a couple of times, he was leaning back, legs crossed, arms outstretched, watching and listening to the laughter of all the children playing.

He fascinated me. Where did he come from? Where was he going? To this day I am sorry that my shyness kept me from asking him, from sitting down next to him and having a long conversation about who he was. Over the years, whenever I feel trapped, I often think of him. He must have represented freedom to me.

The next scene was in church. My wedding day. So clearly as though they were still alive – I saw my father, ill from nephritis, his blue suit, his dark skin, his sad eyes. My bridesmaids were dressed in yellow with yellow picture hats. Mom had a bluish grey lace dress. At the reception I relived dancing with my father-in-law, seeing the ballroom full of people, eating and talking and dancing.

"Why did I marry my husband?" I was asked.

Because no one would help me get out of the engagement. I wanted to go to college but allowed myself to accept an engagement ring. I didn't love him. I wanted to end it but then I didn't know if I would be making a mistake, and would anyone else love me? There was no one to blame. I made those decisions out of fear and confusion. And if I didn't love him and he left me, like Lincoln, I wouldn't suffer as much as I had when Lincoln was killed.

It was time to do more forgiving – of my family. Of myself for agreeing to marry someone I didn't want to. And then I understood, at more profound levels, why I allowed myself in 1996 to the middle of 1997 to live with another man I didn't love. Every day, during those two years, I resolved to love him: He adored me; we square-danced together every Friday night; he was helpful and supportive. What more could I want? I don't know but, every day, I found it impossible.

History had repeated itself. Continuing to lie on the table, I observed the movie playing inside my head, felt the feelings and let them go. I also felt the sadness on my face turn to joy. The corners of my mouth turned upwards and, even though my eyes were closed, I knew they were shining.

# FIRE IN THE KITCHEN

Jerry Della Femina starts out his autobiography, An Italian Grows in Brooklyn, by denying a Prince Spaghetti commercial of school children running home for lunch. He said the Italians never ate lunch at home in the Gravesend section of Brooklyn.

Here in Ithaca, I never had lunch at home either. What I had every school day, between 12:00 and 1:15, was dinner.

No peanut butter and jelly sandwich for Mom's children. They were like four letter words as far as she was concerned. We had spaghetti or stuffed peppers made with eggplant, homemade prosciutto, bread, Romano cheese, tomatoes and of course olive oil and garlic. If it was Friday during Lent, we had baccala (codfish) or spaghetti with clam or lobster sauce or meatless pizza. I always felt sorry for my friends; their vegetables were so unimaginative. I had dandelions, spinach, broccoli or twenty other vegetables sautéed with olive oil and garlic, or tomatoes.

Mom, Louise and I picked the dandelions from open fields seven or eight blocks from home. After filling two or three large paper bags, Mom then spent the rest of the day cleaning, washing and cooking the greens. They were also good in salads with a dressing of olive oil and vinegar.

People are learning once again that dandelion greens are plentiful, cheap, and nutritious. Dandelions support brain and bladder function, digestion, reduce swelling and inflammation, and treat viruses, jaundice, edema, gout, eczema and acne, and prevent cancer. And they were brought to America by Italian immigrants!

---

## ON A SUNDAY AFTERNOON WALK

A serendipitous cache of dandelion greens
on a busy city street
and my life is not only enriched
but transformed.
The lowly is the most significant.
washing and rinsing, washing
and rinsing root, leaf, dead material.
I think of people
spraying poisons on the gold
to acquire cemetery-like lawns.
Earlier that day I asked for and received
relief from back pain.
Used it to bow down in reverence
Before an iron-rich blessing.

~JM

---

Today, Americans eat enormous amounts of sugar and processed salt. When you read food labels, especially for the processed foods that make meals easy to create, the amount of sodium is frightening. If you love sweets, or soft drinks, you're overloading yourself with sugar, and courting diabetes and heart disease. And the aspartame in diet drinks and foods is even worse for you.

As a single mom, when I was back at school, I cooked on the weekends, so my children would have nutritious, home-cooked meals. Couples might cook together on weekends—even get the kids involved.

If there's a CSA in your area, you can get local, organic produce much more cheaply. CSA means "Community Supported Agriculture." A farm will sell shares of its crops. You can sign up for anything from a half-share, for a single person, to several shares for a large family. Every week, the CSA delivers seasonal produce, from spring asparagus to winter squash.

Here are some suggestions by Dr. Khalsa for healthy eating.

1. Buy healthier food.
2. Cook consciously and eat mindfully
3. Eat more fruits and vegetables.
4. Reduce portion size.
5. Shop at farmers' markets.
6. Eat organic produce.
7. Take vitamins and minerals

And here are some of my favorite Italian recipes. Use organic foods whenever possible.

**Begin with a cleansing soak to neutralize pesticides for foods that are not organic.**

| 1 Tbs. | Organic Apple Cider Vinegar |
| 1 Gallon | Water |

Combine, and soak

| Thin leafed vegetables | 5 minutes |
| Thick skinned vegetables and fruits | 10-15 minutes |
| Eggs | 20 minutes |
| Meats | 10-20 minutes/pound |

Rinse thoroughly in cold water.

**Wedding Day Soup**

| 1 | chicken, cut up |
| 1 | large onion, with skin on |
| 1 | large head escarole |

| 1 qt. | canned tomatoes |
| 1 lb. | pasta of your choice |
| grated Romano cheese | |

Place chicken in 8-qt. soup pot. Add onion. Cover with water, no more than 2 inches from top of pot. Cover, and bring to a boil. Reduce and simmer for 2 ½ hours. Remove chicken and onion.

Cool chicken, and remove bones from meat. Wash escarole and tear into pieces. Cook escarole, tomatoes, and meatballs in finished broth at least ½ hour. Boil pasta in separate pot, and add to soup. Add grated cheese to each serving.

See recipe for meatballs. Form thumb-sizes balls.

## Baccala

| 2 lbs. | fresh cod |
| 1 qt. | canned tomatoes |
| 3-4 Tbs. | olive oil |
| 1 clove | garlic, minced |
| 1 | onion, sliced |
| basil | |
| parsley | |

Saute garlic and onion in olive oil until lightly colored (2-3 minutes). Add tomatoes. Bring to a boil, reduce heat, cover, and simmer 30 minutes, stirring often.

Add fish. Cook 30 minutes, or until fish flakes. Serve with chopped basil and/or parsley on top. Season with sea salt and pepper to taste. Mushrooms may be added with the onions and garlic and clams may be substituted for cod. Serves 4.

## Polenta

Polenta is the classic corn meal dish of northern Italy, particularly from the Piedmont region. In this part of the country, polenta is more frequently served than is the pasta of southern Italy. Polenta is prepared in dozens of different ways. Sometimes there are anchovies incorporated into the dish; sometimes cheese and anchovies; and sometimes it is baked with layers of these ingredients. The type of cheese varies according to whatever is on hand or as taste dictates. All of these are suitable as a side dish. There is also the dessert polenta, made with vanilla and sugar. They are all delicious and well worth adding to a cook's repertoire. This is a simple one with cheese.

## Polenta Al Formaggio (Corn Meal with Cheese)

| | |
|---|---|
| 4 C. | water |
| 1 ½ tsp. | salt |
| 1 C. | yellow corn meal |
| 2 C. | Gruyere cheese, grated |
| ¼ stick | butter |

Add the salt to the water in a large saucepan and bring to a boil. Slowly stir in the corn meal, stirring the mixture until it thickens.

Reduce the heat to low, cover the pan, and continue cooking for about 20 minutes. Stir occasionally.

Use additional butter to grease a shallow baking dish. Spread half the cooked corn meal into the baking dish. Spread half the cheese. Dot with half the butter. Spread the remaining corn meal, the remaining cheese, and dot with remaining butter.

Bake in 375 degree oven for 15 minutes, or until top is golden brown. Serves 4.

**Marinated Peppers**

2 or 3     peppers
white vinegar
clove garlic

Cut up peppers. Marinate in solution of half water, half vinegar, and clove of garlic. Refrigerate, checking liquid level, for 2 weeks. For extra flavor, add fresh basil leaves.

**Sauteed Vegetables**

1 lb.     your choice of broccoli, spinach, carrots, cabbage, cauliflower, kale, onions, asparagus, dandelion, of other greens
olive oil
chopped garlic

Saute each of the vegetables in 3-4 tablespoons olive oil and garlic. Amazingly enough, they taste even better when slightly burned.

**Sauteed Vegetables with Tomatoes**

1 qt.     non-seeded, non-peeled tomatoes
sliced mushrooms
sliced, seeded, cut up peppers
green beans
olive oil
chopped garlic
salt and pepper to taste

Saute garlic in olive oil, add tomatoes and one of the vegetables. Bring to a boil, reduce heat, and cook for ½ hour, stirring occasionally. Salt and pepper to taste.

## Gnocchi

| 3 C. | hot mashed potatoes |
|------|---------------------|
| 2 C. | flour |
| 3 Tbs. | Romano cheese, freshly grated |
| 2 | egg yolks |

flour for kneading

Mix all ingredients, except extra flour for kneading, in a bowl. Turn out, and knead in a floured surface until dough is smooth. Pinch off pieces, roll between your palms into half-inch strands. Cut roughly into thumb-sized pieces, then roll each piece down floured fork tines, pressing firmly.

Boil in water 10 minutes, or until Gnocchi rise to the surface. Serve with tomato sauce, meatballs, sausage, and grated Romano cheese. Serves 4.

## Pizza and Sauce

### Sauce:

| 2-3 qt. | canned tomatoes, well drained of juice |
|---------|-----------------------------------------|
| ¼ C. | or a bit more, of olive oil |
| 2-3 | cloves garlic, chopped |
| 2 tsp. | oregano |
| ¼ C. | Romano cheese, freshly grated |

dried basil and parsley, to taste

Bring all ingredients, except cheese, to boil. Reduce heat, cover, and cook 20 minutes. Add cheese.

### Dough

| 1 pkg. | yeast | 1 Tbs. | salt |
|--------|-------|--------|------|
| 1 C. | warm (not hot) water | 2 Tbs. | olive oil |
| 1 Tbs. | sugar | 2 ½ C | unbleached flour |

Dissolve yeast in water. Mix together flour, sugar, and salt. Add to yeast. Add oil, and mix well. Stir in flour. Cover, and let dough rise in a warm place. Grease cookie sheet, and stretch dough out to size of sheet.

Add fresh grated mozzarella cheese to dough, cover with sauce and hot Italian sausage. Toppings could also include fried eggplant, pepperoni, olives. Bake at 350 degrees until the bottom of the dough is brown.

## Italian Meatballs

| | |
|---|---|
| 1 1/2lb. | ground beef |
| 1 | egg |
| 2 Tbs. | fresh parsley, finely chopped |
| 1 clove | garlic, chopped |
| 1 | onion, chopped |
| 3 Tbs. | Romano cheese, grated |
| 1 slice | day old bread, crumbled |
| salt & pepper to taste | |

Mix ingredients well, and roll into 3-4" balls. Add to uncooked tomato sauce, simmer 3 hours, stirring often.

## Tomato Sauce with Meat

| | |
|---|---|
| ¼ C. | olive oil |
| 1 | large onion, sliced |
| 2 cloves | garlic, chopped |
| 28 oz. | tomato puree |
| 28 oz. | water |

In a large, heavy pan, sauté onion and garlic over low heat. Add tomato puree and water, and stir well. Add meatballs, Italian sausage, or other meat. Bring to a boil, then reduce hat to a simmer, cover. Cook about 3 hours, stirring often. Add sea salt and fresh ground pepper to taste.

For a non-meat Christmas Eve dish, Mom added lobster tails to the sauce, instead of the meatballs.

## Italian Stuffed Peppers

| | |
|---|---|
| 6-7 | large peppers, cut in half and seeded |
| 1 | large eggplant, peeled, sliced, diced, and salted; left in colander with water squeezed out |
| ½ loaf | day old Italian bread |
| 1 lb. | Italian sausage, hot, if desired |
| 1 qt. | canned tomatoes, drained |
| olive oil | |
| 2 cloves | chopped garlic |
| ½ C. | Romano cheese, grated |
| salt & pepper to taste | |

In a large bowl, break up the bread, add tomatoes, a little olive oil, sausage, squeezed eggplant, cheese, basil and pepper. Mix well, fill peppers. Place in a greased baking pan, and bake uncovered 350 degrees for 3 hours. Loosen peppers from time to time, pressing filling down. Best to prepare eggplant the day before, or much earlier in the day before baking peppers.

## Chicken Mary

| | |
|---|---|
| 1 | chicken, cut up |
| 1/3 C. | olive oil |
| 2/3 C. | balsamic vinegar |
| 1 Tbs. | oregano |
| 1 Tbs. | basil |
| 2 cloves | garlic, chopped |
| salt & pepper to taste | |

Mix the oil, vinegar, garlic, oregano, and basil in a cup. Place chicken pieces in a heavy, lidded pan. Pour in the sauce and bring to a boil.

Reduce heat, and cover pan tightly. Cook chicken 15 minutes on each side. Good made early in the day so flavors blend. Serve with brown rice, a sautéed vegetable and dessert.

## Frozen Tiramisu

| | |
|---|---|
| 1 C. | strong coffee (from instant is fine) |
| 3 Tbs. | rum (optional) |
| 2 3-oz. pkg. (48) | ladyfingers |
| ½ gallon | coffee ice cream |
| 4 oz. | bittersweet chocolate, grated coarsely |
| 8 oz. | mascarpone cheese |
| 3 Tbs. | coffee-flavored liqueur |
| 1 Tbs. | sugar or honey |
| 1/3 C. | half & half |

Mix coffee and rum together, then line 2 qt. metal loaf type pan with plastic wrap. Using pastry brush, paint coffee/rum mixture onto ladyfingers. Then line pan with ladyfingers, rounded side down. Stir chocolate into ice cream, keeping one-half cup of the chocolate for garnish. Spread ice cream into the loaf pan, using a rubber spatula. Cover with a layer of ladyfingers, and cover with plastic wrap. Freeze for at least 2 hours.

Garnish with a smooth whisked mixture of cheese, liqueur and sugar. Unmold dessert and slice. Drizzle with sauce, and sprinkle with chocolate.

## Sweet Anise Easter Bread

Mom made this every year, and so do I.

| | |
|---|---|
| 1 pkg. | dry yeast |
| ¼ C. | warm water |
| 2/3 C. | sugar |

| ½ C. | milk |
| 1/3 C | butter |
| ½ Tbs. | sea salt |
| 2 Tbs. | anise seed |
| 2 | egg yolks |
| 3 C. | unbleached flour |

Sprinkle yeast and 1 Tbs. sugar into water. Set aside. Heat milk, butter, then pour into t large bowl, and cool. Stir in the yeast, sugar, water mixture. Add egg yolk, and half the flour, and beat one minute at low speed, then 3 minutes at medium speed.

Gradually stir in the rest of the flour to make a soft dough. Knead on a floured surface for 8-10 minutes until smooth and elastic.

Let rise till double in bulk. Punch dough sown, divide into 3 parts, rolling each part between your hands to make a rope. Place into a greased pie plate, sealing the ends together. Place in a warm place, and rise till doubled. Then bake in 350 degree oven about 30 minutes until golden brown, and loaf sounds hollow when tapped. Makes 3 round loaves.

**Ricotta Pie**

| 4 | egg yolks |
| ¾ C. | sugar or honey |
| 2 C. | unbleached flour |
| ½ C. | butter |
| 1 | grated lemon rind |
| 1 Tbs. | water (eliminate if using honey) |

Beat egg yolks, sugar,and add 1 C. flour, butter, and mix well. Add remaining flour, lemon rind, and water. Mix well, but do not over mix. Divide dough in half (dough is thick) and roll out to fit greased 9-inch glass (don't use aluminum) pie plate.

Filling:

| | |
|---|---|
| 1 lb. | ricotta cheese |
| 2 | eggs |
| 1/3 C. | sugar or honey |
| 1 Tbs. | vanilla extract |
| 1 Tbs. | flour |
| 1/2 Tbs. | lemon extract |

Mix all ingredients together, and pour into pie shell. Roll out the other half of the dough, cut into strips. Cover the filling, leaving spaces between the strips for moisture to evaporate. Seal edges of the pie crust with fork tines and cut off excess dough. Bake at 350 degrees for 30 minutes.

**Sour Cream Cookies**

| | |
|---|---|
| 1 C. | brown sugar |
| 2 C. | unbleached flour |
| ½ C | butter |
| ½ Tbs. | nutmeg |
| ½ C. | sour cream |
| ½ Tbs. | baking soda |
| 1 | egg, beaten |
| 2 Tbs. | baking powder |
| ½ Tbs. | salt |
| 1 C. | chopped nuts |

Mix ingredients in order listed. Drop by spoonful on a greased cookie sheet. Bake in a 400 degree oven for 15 minutes. Nuts are optional. Cookies may be sprinkled with sugar before baking.

Dad loved Sour Cream cookies and was most appreciative when I made them for him – which I loved to do. I first tasted them at one of my neighbor's homes: Aunt Mabel. She was my earliest friend's aunt, thus the name. Aunt Mabel was special to me for another reason – she taught me to walk with my toes pointed straight ahead, and not pointed out, like Dad's.

Our good Mother Earth provides everything we need for our bodies and minds to be healthy and in balance. Just as the right foods can be used as medicine, other fruits of the Earth, flower essences and essential oils, can also be our bodies' allies. I dowse to find out which healing essences and supplements will benefit me each day.

# WHAT A WONDERFUL WORLD

In the 1980s flower essences were introduced to me. I was very depressed and couldn't stop worrying about certain things. One worry concerned our government. I don't remember the specifics, but I recall how I tried, over and over, to stop the thoughts without success.

Taking pity on me, Mabel Beggs invited me to her home and told me about Dr. Edward Bach (pronounced *Batch*) and his Flower Essences. Some years earlier while in Europe, she had studied with a woman who had studied with Dr. Bach, an English bacteriologist and pathologist, in the 1930s, who developed the use of flower essences for healing purposes. Dr. Bach is a pioneer in the discovery of how stress and emotions affect illnesses.

Dowsing to determine from which essence I would benefit, Mabel put a specific number of drops of three of four different essences in a one-ounce bottle. She added water and a tiny bit of whiskey to preserve it, and dowsed again to determine how many drops I was to take four times a day.

Amazingly, like turning off a switch or throwing away a bag of garbage, the thoughts disappeared, or ceased, or whatever. I began examining my other worries, and came to the conclusion that they were a waste of time and energy. Of course, with each worry, unreasonable concern, or stressful situation I resolve, another becomes known to me. It is an ongoing process. Flower essences help me.

Flower essences give us, at a vibrational level, the same lift we experience walking in a beautiful garden or into a room filled with lovely blooms. These essences are created by floating flowers at the peak of their bloom in a bowl of pure water and placing them in sunlight. Their healing power is released into the water – the "mother" essence – and is preserved in either brandy or vinegar.

Everything has a distinct vibration, and this is true for our bodies as well. Our "vibrational well-being" is diminished by any dis-ease or disharmony in our physical, emotional, mental, or spiritual systems. Flower essences restore the correct vibration through the principle of resonance. This is the same principle by which one vibrating tuning fork held near a second one will cause that other fork to vibrate as well. By taking a flower essence we benefit from its healing resonance.

Flower essences balance, stabilize, and repair our electrical system, which is intricate and vast beyond scientific comprehension. We do, however, know that every organ and cell of our body is interrelated and activated through this network. Understanding this helps us also understand the important role flower essences play in the field of complementary health care. The electrical pattern of the flower petals is released into the water, which conducts the electricity, and the resulting flower essence water is used to stabilize and repair the body's electrical system.

Flower essences can be purchased online, by local practitioners, or at some natural food stores. It's best to begin using flower essences with a trained practitioner.

\* \* \*

Along with flower essences, I also use essential oils. I learned about them from Emma and Don Harner, good friends who I met when square dancing. Don and Emma distribute a brand of essential oils made by a company whose owner, Gary Young, has a compelling story about how and why he makes these products.

He grew up on a farm in Idaho. At 17, he moved to Canada to begin a career in logging and ranching. When he was 24, a logging accident left him in a coma for three weeks; then paralyzed and confined to a wheelchair. The doctor told him he would never walk again. Gary began researching and using essential oils for his pain. Thirteen years after the accident he ran his first half marathon. Now he researches, develops, and creates essential oils to help others to heal.

I find Gary Young's story inspiring. Like me, he took back his life from the physicians, and found a way to heal himself, physically, emotionally, and spiritually. Too often, people accept what a doctor tells them and give up. Both Gary's philosophy and his life show us the importance of taking responsibility for our own healing and health.

 ===== HAPPY TO BE HERE =====

Flashback to 1977. As my left leg collapsed under me, causing me to pitch forward down the steps and land face down in a bed of myrtle and mint (at least I smelled good from the experience) I saw in my mind's eye two toothpicks snapping apart in the warm breeze. Terrified, I picked myself up, brushed myself off, amazed that I wasn't bruised or banged up or sore in any part of my body, changed my clothes and set off on my errands that took me out in the warm July morning in the first place.

"Why did this happen?" was the silent litany I asked over and over as I clutched stair railings, or descended my second floor, 17-step staircase backwards, feeling 102 rather than the healthy, energetic 60-year-old that I was. It could happen again. Anytime.

So I made an appointment with my nutritionist/allergist/ reflexologist to explore the cause. Then my philosophy of believing I could heal myself kicked back in. In bed at the time, I turned to a book on my night table and within minutes discovered that I had been poisoning my body every morning and evening—and sometimes in between—with fluoride in the toothpaste.

What I'm going to relate next will seem like a lie, but I swear it's the truth. Hanna Kroeger, author of *God Helps Those Who Help Themselves*, has her book on illness and holistic healing divided up into seven sections; one on each of the seven causes for ill health. It was included in a pile of books a friend had recently given me to peruse. Perhaps they could be useful in a library devoted to biodynamic living. The title, at first, didn't thrill me. Now I thank goodness that I overlooked it and opened the book. To my delight, I found a warm, loving, incredibly knowledgeable trained nurse who is a pioneer in health foods and self-healing.

Not having read the book from cover to cover, nevertheless I was aware of some of the sections and categories. In my hands, the book opened, not to the table of contents, or the section on worms and parasites as a cause of ill health, but in the middle where *Chapter IV, Metals and Other Poisons* as a cause of ill health, is located. As I read, my hand went up to my mouth, in disbelief and relief.

Not total disbelief. I knew from conversations with my nutritionist that fluoride may cause allergies. I was amazed to learn from this book that all the pain I had been experiencing could also be related to fluoride poisoning. The excruciating backaches with which I had been waking up every morning, the feeling that my legs would collapse under me at any moment, the fact that I couldn't ride my exercise bike that winter, and that I needed a crutch to lean on the prior summer because my right leg muscles hurt so much—these were all symptoms of possible fluoride poisoning.

My nutritionist confirmed my fears. Knowledge is a powerful antidote for me, so I'm certain it worked as fast as the food supplements I took to detox my system. Within days, my legs felt strong and my fear of falling disappeared. Over the ensuing three months I was able to start exercising again. Even today I can easily walk the mile and a half it takes to go and return from the nearest store that carries fluoride-free toothpaste.

# HELLO OLD FRIENDS

As I've mentioned so often, all matter is energy, and energy carries vibration. Negative thoughts and worries, unhealthy beliefs that we learn from society, and environmental toxins all can lower our energy and vibrations, leading to physical, emotional, and spiritual illness.

There are therapists, medical intuitives, who can tune our energy vibrations, even from a distance. I learned about such healers, sometimes called "sensitives," from my chiropractor Bernie Graham, whose wife Madeline is an energy healer.

My friend Dorothy Lonsky, who is one of the connectors in my life, introduced me to one such healer, Deena Spear. Dorothy made kefir for Deena, and took me with her on a delivery to Deena's home in nearby Trumansburg.

After 25 years as a violinmaker, Deena discovered she could adjust the sound of an instrument without tools, or without even touching it. Eventually she could adjust clients' instruments over the telephone. From there, she began to use the same tuning skills for humans.

Deena has a wonderful sense of humor about her work. Writing about how she learned to become a healer, she says:

> "I wrote *Ears of the Angels* to describe my not-particularly-graceful [shift] from respected (or at least we thought so) violin maker (my husband and I worked with high level musicians) to I'm not sure what (fruit loop perhaps?) acoustical healer."

Speaking of a higher vibrational energy, this is a good place to mention sound healing. Sound Healing can heal physical and psychic pain, and improve mental clarity. Kate Payne, at the Foundation of Light, created tapes with sounds that will help to heal various spiritual and physical difficulties. I used them often in my healing journey.

It's important to have self-awareness as well as an awareness of environmental factors and toxins that sap our mental and physical energy, and to use every possible method to avoid or block those negative influences

## DANCING IN THE STREETS

With my newfound energy, I could square dance with joy. Angeles Arrien writes, "Every culture in the world has singing, dancing, and storytelling, and these are practices to which we all have access." To those three things, she adds silence and listening. Singing, dancing, storytelling, and silence—these are an important part of my healing journey.

> *If there's no dancing*
> *at the revolution,*
> *I'm not coming.*
> ~ Emma Goldman

\* \* \*

Teacup Chain is one of my favorite square dance calls. It requires knowledge and the active participation of all eight dancers in the square. The steps change, depending on whether one is dancing as a head couple or a side couple, and it had been six years since I'd last attended a club dance.

What shined my black dancing shoes on Sunday, October 24, 2004, was that *I remembered the steps.*

\* \* \*

Knowing all the harm stress causes I am still learning how to stop worrying. You can do it, too. When I write that we simply need to stop worrying, I am not implying that it will be easy. What I mean to say is that if a person says he or she wants to be well, then a commitment must be made to examine the sources of the problem, find non-drug help if needed, and make the necessary changes.

Responses like "It is easier said than done," or, "I have children," or, "It is too hard," or, "I don't know how," or, "Our whole life is full of stress," won't work. Those are examples of cyclic thinking, of lack of self-awareness and emotional maturity. They weaken our resolve.

> *We defy the laws of humanity by conscious direction of our awareness and energy. That is the depth of commitment.*
> - Barbara Marciniak

If we are intelligent, loving, contributing members of society—in other words, not hypocritical, or victims, or dishonest, or lazy—we understand that we are responsible for our well-being. And so we take the time to become aware of our sources of anxiety and concerns, and put our money where our mouths are.

## REAL SECURITY

The Madwoman of Chaillot said that to be happy, one must make lists every morning.

| The "No" List | The "Yes" List |
|---|---|
| 1) Cigarettes | 1) Never needed them |
| 2) New clothes | 2) Beautiful items at rummage sales & vintage |
| 3) Panty hose | 3) Wear slacks |
| 4) Long-distance phone calls | 4) Write letters |
| 5) Makeup | 5) Smile more |
| 6) Paid entertainment | 6) Be a volunteer usher |
| 7) Paper napkins, towels | 7) Use cloth |
| 8) Clothes dryer | 8) Hang up the wash |
| 9) Meals out | 9) Do potlucks |
| 10) Processed foods | 10) Cook from scratch |
| 11) Alcohol | 11) Never needed it |
| 12) Soda | 12) Water or juice |
| 13) Unnecessary driving | 13) Walk for exercise |

 HAPPY DAYS ARE HERE AGAIN

In the 1940s and 50s, being seen at a rummage sale was almost as bad as being seen in jail. But, with many other attitudes in our culture, that has changed. I love rummage sales. They are like treasure hunts or birthday parties where your friends and neighbors are invited, and the wonderful surprises that you find for—well, not pennies any more, but very little—are like gifts.

I go now for fun, for a book, or an antique. Like one Thursday at the Methodist church sale.

In the church basement, tables were overflowing with housewares, Christmas decorations, crafts, books, jewelry, electronics, clothes, bedding. To me, the sale appeared to be the largest I had ever seen there.

While looking around, going from table to table, seeing what I already have or don't want to make room for in my life, and deciding that it was time to leave, I suddenly picked up a black mug. Turning it around in my hand, reading the white-lettered words, I understood why I had come.

What seems
like only a
ripple today . . .
can become
the wave of
the future.

LISTENING

depression is a stopped clock
it's the absence of light
it's carrying around one hundred pound sacks
of anger, anxiety, sorrow and guilt
and climbing all your mountains
encased in cement

depression is incurable
some doctors tell you
it's inherited and familial
the filmmakers and drug pushers say
it's eleven million strong the statisticians repeat
year after year
children are not allowed
fifty years behind the times for me
it's my fault
it's not my fault

do something

if living well is a craft
what do i use for tools
or material
all around me melancholy people
stay that way

withered grape vines
their whole lives through
who are my models

drugs are the answer
drugs are the problem
how can i learn to walk
on legs full only of sawdust
or use a mind badly leaking hope

i left a trail
    unhappy childhood
    miserable teenhood
    abusive marriage
    divorce no real help
    motherhood a tragedy
    christianity a myth
    education arrogance
that ended in a darkened room
    beyond despair
    beyond exhaustion
    beyond repair
    or so i thought

unfelt hands lifted me
unknown source of energy
ballooned my legs
oiled my arms
nodded my head
yes
to improved food
for thought
and deed
to alternative therapies
for subconscious learning

*Jemma Macera*

to shaman rituals
for banishing negative
cultural and karmic spirits

i learned
there are no absolutes
illness is a gift
teaching us
patience
kindness
truthfulness
simplicity
ecstasy
that you and i
and the goddess
are one.
~JM

# PUT A LITTLE LOVE IN YOUR HEART

"What is *real*?" asked the Rabbit one day, when they were lying side by side near the nursery fender, before Anna came to tidy the room. "Does it mean having things that buzz inside you and a stick-out handle?"

"Real isn't how you are made," said the Skin Horse. "It's a thing that happens to you. When a child loves you for a long, long time, not just to play with, but *really* loves you, then you become Real."

"Does it hurt?" asked the Rabbit.

"Sometimes." said the Skin Horse, for he was always truthful. "When you are Real you don't mind being hurt."

"Does it happen all at once, like being wound up," he asked, "or bit by bit?"

"It doesn't happen all at once," said the Skin Horse. "You become. It takes a long time. That's why it doesn't often happen to people who break easily, or have sharp edges, or who have to be carefully kept. Generally, by the time you are Real, most of your hair has been loved off, and your eyes drop out and you get loose in the joints and very shabby. But these things don't matter at all because once you are Real, you can't be ugly, except to people who don't understand."

-from *The Velveteen Rabbit*

 CLIMB EVERY MOUNTAIN

Just as grapes
use cool nights
in late summer
to sweeten

We have cold experiences
and long dark nights
to understand. ~JM

If we are to heal ourselves of any dis-ease, dis-harmony, be it dementia, depression, schizophrenia, a cold, cerebral palsy or cancer, we must own our life, our experiences. External life is really an outward manifestation of an internal reality. Most people refuse to accept the connection, disassociate themselves from the un-favorable conditions, see themselves as victims, and turn to professionals who support and re-enforce that position with treatments that only prolong the bell tolling for thee.

Life's journey is a spiral. Perhaps it was the theologian Pierre Teilhard de Chardin who first introduced that concept to me. Movement on that upward path is forwards and backwards at the same time. Quantum physics is discovering that truth at subatomic levels. Therefore, if we repeatedly find ourselves in and out of depression or one of its many variations, it is because we are not learning the lessons life has set out for us in order to become happy, healthy, productive members of the Universe. We are, in effect, stuck: emotionally, psychologically, culturally, anthropologically, spiritually, nutritionally, evolutionarily, and more.

Life will support us in all and every effort we make to become truly human. We have to be willing to be bold. Goethe said "there is genius in boldness." (Do not make the mistake of equating boldness with rudeness, arrogance or immaturity.) We have to be willing to take the risks, question authority that says something can't be done. That was one of the most important lessons I learned on my pilgrimage of healing.

Of absolute necessity we must first love ourselves. Then we must seek out the particular types of counseling and therapy we need to give us the self-awareness and the decision making abilities we need to grow into the human-ness that learns life's lessons without the pain and suffering of this culture.

Pain is the result of hanging on to the experience. Because most everyone we know experiences pain, is in pain of some sort, we subconsciously use them as models, thus perpetuating the myths.

It has taken me a library of books, a sea of words, years of searching, un-learning, re-learning, questioning, trying, believing and believing and believing that I can be well to achieve that goal (I'm still learning).

It was Ben Franklin who said only a fool has himself for a teacher. Therefore we must seek out authorities and question authorities almost simultaneously. And because wellness is a many splendored thing, quality help in a multiplicity of areas is needed.

In depression it is the nervous system that has to be healed. Jeanne Achterberg, Ph. D., says we have up to a trillion nerve endings. Contrary to popular belief, nutrition does play a most significant role. But it is a healthy, daily diet that is needed. Not the massive overloading of certain vitamins that get prescribed like drugs and are either eliminated by the body or stored in body fat, causing potential harm.

Dr. Achterberg also points out that research has discovered the brain's ability to visualize is not limited to one area, such as many other functions are. This is indicative of the important role the imagination plays in healing ourselves and others.

Emotional maturity which comes, in part, from self-awareness which leads to responsible behavior is of vital importance to gain understanding about how our energies are being used and mis-used: energies drained by anger, anxieties, guilt, grief, and physical pain.

Rest, relaxation, creativity to satisfy deeper soul levels is another absolute. It can be friends, theatre, quiet time, painting, bowling, or chain saw sculpting. No matter. Find out what satisfies and pursue your bliss, as Joseph Campbell urges.

One issue I came to understand through my pain, is that prescription drugs are no different than illegal drugs. They both kill. The difference is time. That's not to say medicine isn't useful. Good medicine. Friends are good medicine. Joy is good medicine. Joy in the form of laughter healed the author Norman Cousins of a terminal dis-ease.

The world renowned psychiatrist, Dr. Carl Jung, has told us that true healing, transformation, comes from understanding that man/woman is 2,000,000 years old. Therefore what is interpreted as genetics can many times be experiences stored in body cells and tissue. Layers and layers and layers of cells. Once again the Universe has provided us with unusual people with incredible healing techniques to help those of us wishing to be well.

Trager therapy, Sacral-Cranial therapy, Polarity, Reflexology, Rolfing (Structural Integration therapy), Bach remedies, authentic Shaman rituals are just a few. Oh yes, and prayer.

## SHAMAN'S SONG

pray for your enemies
love them
they transform before your eyes
becoming teachers
playing the needed roles
showing us we are interchangeable chessmen
on a cosmic board
sometimes wonderful
sometimes not
always equal.
~JM

CPSIA information can be obtained at www.ICGtesting.com
Printed in the USA
BVOW07s1207240914

368051BV00002B/2/P